Praise for

The Darkness Has Not Overcome

"I worked closely with Cliff Sims every day when I served as Director of National Intelligence. In this book, Cliff gives readers a rare look into a world that most people only see in movies about the White House, or in spy novels—and he does it while providing practical faith lessons that apply to all of our lives."

—John Ratcliffe, Former Director of National Intelligence

"Politics is a cutthroat but ultimately temporal game, and Cliff Sims has played it at the highest level. *The Darkness Has Not Overcome* is full of indispensable lessons on how to view politics through an eternal lens while also being good stewards of the political freedoms we enjoy."

—J.D. Vance, U.S. Senator, *New York Times* bestselling author of *Hillbilly Elegy*

"American Christians are under attack every day by leftwing activists, mainstream media outlets, and liberal politicians who want to take away our most basic freedoms. My friend Cliff Sims has been through the fire and lived to tell about it. *The Darkness Has Not Overcome* is an inspiring read that you'll come back to again and again when you're going through your own challenges." **—Donald Trump, Jr.**

"How does a Christian live with decency in a political world? First, by never forgetting that our fight is not against flesh and blood. We're actors in a larger drama that we can rarely see, but often, if we're quiet enough, can feel very clearly. Cliff Sims understands this, and he's written about it beautifully in this wonderful book."   **—Tucker Carlson**

"American Christians are in an existential fight for liberty and Biblical truth against radical leftwing forces hellbent on undermining both. Cliff Sims has been an indispensable leader in this fight, which is why *The Darkness Has Not Overcome* is a must-read for anyone who wants to preserve the Judeo-Christian values that made America the most special country on Earth."
                    —Charlie Kirk, Founder of Turning Point USA

"Cliff Sims has written the book America has been waiting for. It's nonfiction that reads like a thriller. And in the genre of 'Faith & Politics,' it may be the best book ever written. *The Darkness Has Not Overcome* is a gift to us all—and one you will be anxious to share with everyone you know."
                    —Andy Andrews, *New York Times* bestselling author of
                                    The Traveler's Gift* and *The Noticer

The Darkness Has Not Overcome

Lessons on Faith and Politics from
Inside the Halls of Power

CLIFF SIMS

Former Special Assistant to President Trump
& Deputy Director of National Intelligence

NEW YORK—NASHVILLE

Worthy Books
Hachette Book Group
1290 Avenue of the Americas, New York, NY 10104
Worthypublishing.com
twitter.com/worthybooks

First Edition: May 2024

Worthy Books is a division of Hachette Book Group, Inc. The Worthy Books name and logo are trademarks of Hachette Book Group, Inc.

The publisher is not responsible for websites (or their content) that are not owned by the publisher.

The Hachette Speakers Bureau provides a wide range of authors for speaking events. To find out more, go to hachettespeakersbureau.com or email HachetteSpeakers@ hbgusa.com.

Worthy Books may be purchased in bulk for business, educational, or promotional use. For information, please contact your local bookseller or the Hachette Book Group Special Markets Department at special.markets@hbgusa.com.

Library of Congress Cataloging-in-Publication Data

Names: Simms, Cliff, author.
Title: The darkness has not overcome : lessons on faith and politics from inside the halls of power / Cliff Simms, Former Special Assistant to the President & Deputy Director of National Intelligence.
Description: First edition. | New York : Worthy Books, 2024.
Identifiers: LCCN 2023052699 | ISBN 9781546006596 (hardcover) | ISBN 9781546006619 (ebook)
Subjects: LCSH: Christianity and politics—United States—History. | Religion and politics—United States—History. | Polarization (Social Sciences)—United States—History. | Christian life—United States—History.
Classification: LCC BR115.P7 S5233 2024 | DDC 261.7—dc23/eng/20240124
LC record available at https://lccn.loc.gov/2023052699

ISBNs: 9781546006596 (hardcover), 9781546006619 (ebook)

Printed in the United States of America

LSC-C

Printing 1, 2024

To Shep: It's far better to be a godly man than a great man. Let your light shine.

—Daddy

CONTENTS

PROLOGUE

On March 22, 2017, the leaders of the Congressional Black Caucus (CBC) came to the White House to meet with President Trump for the first time since he'd taken office two months earlier. There were seven members of Congress present, all of them Democrats, none of them Trump supporters.

The weather outside was beautiful, and I had lingered by the Rose Garden a little longer than usual on my way into work that morning. Waiting in the Cabinet Room for the meeting to begin, I took my usual position behind the president's chair to his left.

Another White House aide sat down to my right. "What's up, brother?" he whispered. "It's quiet in here."

He was right; it was very quiet. There was a nervous tension in the air. On the other side of the room, the seven Democratic members of Congress were speaking to one another in hushed tones, and the handful of Trump aides weren't talking at all.

In the summer of 2016, Trump had traveled to Michigan for a campaign stop in Dimondale, just outside of Lansing. Speaking directly to black voters, Trump unloaded on what he described as the failed policies of Democratic politicians. "You're living in poverty, your schools are no good, you have no jobs, fifty-eight percent of your youth [are] unemployed." And then he delivered the line that became most associated with his pitch to black Americans: "What...do you have to lose?" Many Democrats were incensed by the implication that they didn't care about black voters, a core constituency.

These Democrats hadn't forgotten, even seven months later. When they showed up at the White House, they were carrying thick binders prominently titled "We Have a Lot to Lose." The stage seemed to be set for a contentious meeting.

But when the president arrived he seemed to be in a good mood. Trump prided himself on his ability to charm visitors—any visitors, from dictators to CEOs to factory workers. And to his credit, he usually could.

"Hello, everybody," he said with a smile as he breezed into the room.

"Good afternoon, Mr. President," replied CBC chairman Cedric Richmond. Richmond was a four-term congressman from Louisiana's Second Congressional District. A New Orleans native, in addition to being a seasoned legislator, he was a former college baseball player and a polished communicator. He would later become a top White House aide to President Joe Biden.

As the president sat down, the rest of the group followed his lead, and Congressman Richmond presented the president with the CBC's "130-page policy document" meant to educate him and his administration "on the difficult history of black people in this country, the history of the CBC, and solutions to advance black families in the twenty-first century." The president accepted it and promised his staff would dig through it. Then the group discussed ways to bring down the costs of prescription drugs. They chatted about the importance of historically black colleges and universities. They expressed mutual support for rebuilding the country's crumbling infrastructure and revitalizing urban communities.

Trump was Trump. He was open and direct, and spoke in a way that made it clear he had no filter between the thoughts in his head and the words coming out of his mouth. I can't imagine the CBC members had ever experienced an encounter with any president remotely close to this. They may have found it strange, but I'd also guess it was refreshing. Before long they came to the same realization I had seen so many others come to: it's pretty much impossible to spend one-on-one time with Donald Trump and not end up liking him.

In about twenty minutes, the atmosphere had completely shifted from anxious to relaxed. They talked, shared ideas, and laughed together.

At one point in the meeting, Congressman Richmond said something to the president directly that stunned everyone in the room.

"Mr. President," he began slowly, "I believe you have the ability to be one of the best presidents this nation has ever had."

Whoa, I thought, leaning forward in my seat.

"I mean that," he continued. "I don't always agree with the things you say. In fact, sometimes I think you say things that you don't even realize are offensive. But I also think there's something special about you. And I want to work with you to make your presidency a success."

It seemed like the kind of earnestness that is rarely heard across party lines in Washington, D.C.

"I'd love that, Cedric," the president said as he stood up, extended his arm across the table, and shook Richmond's hand. Trump had a triumphant look—he'd talked again and again about how he wanted to meet with the CBC, and now it looked like it was paying off. He believed he shared policy views with black voters, if only they'd give him a chance.

As the meeting broke up, a CBC staffer told me they wanted to hold a press gaggle outside the West Wing to discuss what happened in the meeting. This was a routine request, one we'd allowed for other groups, and we agreed to help facilitate it. As a White House press aide alerted the media and gathered them outside, I continued to chat with the CBC members and their staff in the West Wing lobby. Everyone was in good spirits, and they seemed hopeful that this was the beginning of a positive working relationship with the president and his staff. After all, there were a number of issues on which the CBC and Trump could find agreement. If the members would just say that—that this was a good start—it would be a huge win. I, for one, was pleasantly surprised by how it all seemed to be coming together.

Once outside and standing in front of a large group of reporters in front of the West Wing, Congressman Richmond expressed his appreciation to the president for taking the time to meet, calling it "a meeting where both sides listened." He called the president "receptive" and said, "The surprising part was that when we talked about the goals, there were more similarities than there were differences." He also said he looked forward to "further engagement on a consistent basis."

So far, so good.

But then he departed from that script. He claimed to have confronted the president about some of his past comments about President Obama. I looked over at the CBC's communications aide. That topic had never even come up during the meeting.

Then came the question everyone had been waiting for.

"[The president's] been accused of being a racist, a bigot..." a reporter said. "Coming out of this meeting with him, do you believe those things to be true?"

The meeting had gone so well, and Congressman Richmond had been so sincere and complimentary of him behind closed doors, I thought he might at least be willing to say he didn't personally believe Trump was racist. But he didn't.

The best he would do is to say, "He's the forty-fifth president of the United States..."

I looked over at the CBC press aide, who was standing right beside me. The subtle smirk on his face reminded me of a card shark at the moment he revealed his winning hand to a befuddled mark.

I whispered to him, "After everything he said in that meeting when no cameras were around, he's still going to stand in front of the White House and suggest the president might be racist?"

He shrugged, then made a dismissive comment about another White House aide with whom they'd had a contentious relationship, as if the sudden reversal were all her fault.

With that, what started as a hopeful effort to improve race relations was officially crushed under the weight of hard feelings, pettiness, mistrust, and the cynicism of Washington, D.C.

The entire episode was a microcosm of what goes on in our nation's capital every day. In my experience, very little of what the public sees is an accurate reflection of what goes on behind closed doors. Everyone seems to have an ulterior motive or self-serving agenda. The smiles of the preening politicians mask the cutthroat, cunning ambition for power that simmers just below the surface. The handshakes and backslaps from the lobbyists and consultants distract from their single-minded pursuit of wealth and the fact that they'll never take your call again once you're not in a position to help them attain it.

There are, of course, exceptions to these rules. In many ways, President Trump was one of them. There is no "private" Trump; what you see is what you get. If he says something publicly, you can rest assured that he's been railing about the same thing privately. For anyone trying to make sense of his rise and staying power, it's really this simple: authenticity is so rare in American life that when someone is just fully themselves—warts and all—for the entire world to see, it resonates.

Never mind the political implications of this; how about the spiritual implications? For every phony politician, we have a phony television pastor or evangelist basically telling the same story: donate your money to me and your life will dramatically improve!

In fact, American politics and the American church have more in common than we'd like to admit. And if the church looks just like the world, what does it really have to offer?

When you think about it that way, it's no wonder that the number of Americans self-identifying as Christians has dropped[1] from 90 percent to 64 percent over the last fifty years and church membership has dropped below 50 percent[2] for the first time ever. Meanwhile, the number of Americans self-identifying as atheists, agnostics, or "nothing in particular" has shot up to 30 percent and, if current trends continue, will become the majority in the decades ahead.

If the quickest way to erode the American church and stifle the spread of the Gospel is to mirror American culture (which is currently consumed by politics), then it stands to reason that the surest way to revive the American church is for us as individuals—and the church as an institution—to embrace being a countercultural movement that stands in stark contrast to everything we see happening around us.

The stakes could not be higher, both in terms of souls being lost for eternity, and for the society in which we now live.

The Root of Our Problem

The late Harvard Business School professor Clayton Christensen once recalled a conversation he had with a Marxist economist from China. He asked the man if he'd learned anything that surprised him during his time in the United States, and he immediately responded, "Yeah, I had no idea how critical religion is to the functioning of democracy. The reason why democracy works," he continued, "is not because the government was designed to oversee what everybody does, but rather democracy works because most people, most of the time, voluntarily choose to obey the law...Americans followed these rules because they had come to believe that they were not just accountable to society, they were accountable to God."

Professor Christensen recalled being struck by the suddenly obvious realization "that as religion loses its influence over the lives of Americans, what will happen to our democracy?...Because if you take away religion, you can't hire enough police."

So much of modern American life is focused on perceived problems that, in reality, are just symptoms of much deeper issues. Social strife, widespread drug addiction, civil unrest, violence, the never-ending allure of power and prestige. The faux outrage of cable news pundits and the incessant anger and condescension that fuels debates on X (formerly known as Twitter). The vanity that drives our social media personae. Activists openly calling for anyone associated with their political opponents to never again be allowed to live in peace. It's almost like the entire nation has descended into an ends-justify-the-means dystopia.

These are all societal problems, sure. But really they are heart problems. Sin problems. The kind of problems that can't be fixed by politicians, pundits, or even preachers. And yet we don't seem to have a framework for how to address these issues because society has decided there isn't even such a thing as objective truth that could be used to decide issues of right and wrong, good and evil. Phrases like "live your truth" and "I'm just speaking my truth" have replaced the Truth—God's Truth—with excuses and lies dressed up in the flowery language of personal empowerment.

As Christians, we have "*the* way, *the* truth, and *the* life" (John 14:6; emphasis added), but everything about it—especially the idea that there is only one way, one truth, and one path to eternal life—is offensive to a culture that insists that everything is relative; that however you "identify" trumps the identity we all have from being formed in the image of God; that whatever makes you superficially happy must be good.

As faith—once central to the American idea—erodes more and more from everyday life in our country, believers who stand firm against moral relativism will see the fulfillment of Christ's declaration in Matthew 10:22 that "you will be hated by all for my name's sake." Or in the parlance of the day, you might just find yourself getting "canceled." Fortunately, we can also find hope in his very next sentence: "But the one who endures to the end will be saved."

This is a book about walking through the fire. But more specifically, it is a book about a unique moment in American life in which politics has consumed everything. Even our churches are tearing themselves apart, not over disagreements about fundamental tenets of our faith, but over political candidates, cultural flashpoints, and debates about whether certain pastors are vessels for the Holy Spirit or an unholy political agenda.

So how should Christians approach our lives in this time of dramatic change and upheaval, when even our church families are in the midst of the strife and division, rather than being a refuge from it? The principles and lessons I'll share here are hard-earned, many of them taken from my own experiences—and failings—working in the most high-pressure political environments on Earth: the White House and the United States Intelligence Community.

A friend of mine with whom I have spent a lot of time in the Middle East recently traveled from her country to my home state of Alabama to speak to local churches about the experiences of persecuted Christians abroad. She began by detailing the persecution she had endured in her country.

When she was growing up, teachers ridiculed her because she had a Christian name and made her sit in the back of the classroom. Neighbors continually tried to shut down her father's shop, depriving her family of a steady living. Others in her city threatened to pour acid on her face and kill members of her family. They stole her family's land. And the police and courts repeatedly refused to protect or defend them.

Toward the end of one church service, a pastor asked her, "How can Christians in America pray for Christians in the

Middle East?" Her answer left the congregation, many of whom are accustomed to their comfortable lives, sitting in stunned silence: but it's becoming more and more relevant to life in our own country.

"Do not pray for the persecution to stop," she said, "because the church is growing when our enemies see how we love them anyway. Instead, pray that God gives us the strength and courage to endure it so that he will be glorified."

She then opened her Arabic Bible to Exodus 1:12 and translated aloud: "But the more they were oppressed, the more they multiplied..."

"Wake up," she said. "Don't be sleepy believers. Don't be a sleepy church. Don't just do the 'normal routine.' There is no time to waste."

These are trying times. Just like refiners purify precious metals through high temperatures, God wants to use the challenging circumstances he puts us in to purify our hearts. "This light momentary affliction is preparing for us an eternal weight of glory beyond all comparison," 2 Corinthians 4:17 says. Proverbs 17:3 tells us, "The crucible is for silver, and the furnace is for gold, and the Lord tests hearts." Through it all, his divine plan is for us to grow less and less reliant on ourselves and more and more reliant on him.

So especially in the darkest days, "let your light shine before others, so that they may see your good works and give glory to your Father who is in heaven" (Matthew 5:16).

Author's Note:
An Opportunity for the Outcasts

Rage

If I'm going to impart some sort of wisdom or "lessons" I've learned in the halls of power, you should first know that my earliest lessons were learned far away from those supposedly hallowed halls.

The first time I remember punching somebody, I was about nine years old. The lesbian prostitutes living next door weren't home—on weekends they rarely were—but their two boys were in their kitchen rolling grass and pine straw in a napkin, trying to smoke it. It wasn't going well.

I thought the whole idea was stupid, and the more I said it the madder it made another neighborhood boy who was egging them on. At some point he tried to push me out the front door and close it, but I held it open with my foot like a rubber doorstop. When he finally stopped pushing, I shoved the door back open and punched him in the mouth. Everyone froze.

The boy held his hand over his lip, and the other two boys peered through the kitchen doorway with their mouths open, pausing their useless attempts to light up their homemade cigarette. Then all three rushed toward me, sending me sprinting back toward my house, jumping the chest-high fence separating our yards, and slamming the front door shut just in time before busting out laughing.

When I was a kid, our neighborhood in south Jackson, Mississippi, was a blast. There was the aspiring cartoonist next door on the other side who taught me how to draw. I didn't know that his wife was in the process of embezzling cash from the church day care where she worked. There was the little boy across the street who'd let me play Sonic the Hedgehog on his Sega Genesis. I didn't know his dad was a drug dealer. There was the park we loved behind our house, with a concrete spillway that we'd ride our bikes through like we were competing in the X Games. We didn't realize the syringes and needles littering the ground weren't from a doctor's office.

But in retrospect there was also a subtle sense of danger, even among us blissfully ignorant kids. Like the time we used water guns to "ambush" a car that was driving by, only to dive into ditches moments later when the driver threw it in reverse and skidded off the road trying to run us over.

Our neighborhood shops even got some unwanted national media attention when, as the *Washington Post* would tell it, "a sniper holed up in an abandoned, burning restaurant sprayed a busy shopping area with gunfire today, killing one person and wounding four others before perishing in the flames...More than 100 shots were fired...during the hour-long siege that forced motorists to crouch behind their cars."[1]

I always thought the occasional gunshots at night were just firecrackers, so it wasn't like I was going to bed scared, but I did have a series of recurring dreams that each ended with me waking up sweating in fear.

The worst one of all began with a witch-like figure, cloaked in black and standing on a hill surrounded by sheep. Then, I would suddenly be in my room, lying in bed in the pitch dark. Hopping up, I would run into my parents' room, where they were sleeping. I'd tap my dad on the shoulder to wake him up, but when he'd roll over it would be the faceless witch, who'd silently lift up the covers and signal for me to "come here" with the slow movement of a bony index finger. I'd hopelessly crawl in and let the covers be pulled over my head before finally waking up shaking. I must have had that dream a hundred times, along with several others.

We didn't have much, but my brother and I had two things going for us that the rest of the neighborhood didn't. We had an incredible mother and father who loved us, took a deep interest in every aspect of our lives, and raised us in a Christian home. And we had grandparents who saved up to send us to a nearby private school. That family, faith, and educational foundation would ultimately set our lives on a different trajectory from the other kids.

But while I never fell into the alcohol, drugs, or full-fledged juvenile delinquency of some of my friends, I never quite shook the chip on my shoulder, even as my family rose into the middle class and my life's journey later took me to places I never would have imagined. In particular, I was filled with an unexplainable rage during my teenage and early college years and had a seemingly innate predilection for violence, which manifested itself in various ways.

Sometimes it was slapping the kid who bullied my younger brother at the bus stop, just so I could embarrass him in front of everyone. Other times it was punching my high school baseball teammate—in the dugout, in the middle of practice—for hitting on my girlfriend. Even among my friend group, disputes were resolved by someone saying "get the gloves," which meant putting on raggedy boxing gloves, going out in the street no matter what time of day or night, and fighting it out until somebody gave up.

Another time it was an all-out brawl with a grown man in his thirties who was dating my friend's mom. He was so drunk one night that when someone dared him to put his hand on a red-hot stovetop, he actually did it. He apparently couldn't feel the pain as we stood in stunned silence, listening to his skin sizzle like bacon. When another friend of mine walked through the front door—clueless to the insanity taking place inside—and cracked a joke, the maniac took his hand off the stove, bum-rushed him, and put him in a chokehold.

As my confused friend flailed with his eyes bulging out of his head, total chaos broke out. Fists flew, furniture toppled over, and the drunken adult pulled out a knife in an attempt to regain control of the situation. It didn't work. By that point we already assumed we were in a struggle for survival and we couldn't lose. Somehow no one was seriously injured as we rushed him and held him down on the floor, still squirming to break free. In the end, the knife was wrested away, and he was restrained like an unhinged mental asylum patient in a movie.

On another occasion, gunfire broke out in a nightclub we were all too young to get into, prompting me and a few friends to take off running toward my car several blocks away. As horrified partiers flooded into the streets, so too did the police who were trying to apprehend the gunman.

As we made it to my car, out of breath from sprinting, our relief quickly turned to terror with the words, "Hands up!" We were briefly blinded by a plainclothes police officer's flashlight, and as we blinked to regain our vision, we each saw the black nine-millimeter pistol pointing at us, one after another. The officer's hands were shaking uncontrollably. I had just started considering how I would explain the butterfly knife in my pocket when a sudden rustling beside my car caused us all to jump, including the police officer.

Unbeknownst to us, the shooter from inside the club had tried to hide between my car and a thin line of trees. But realizing that one officer had already gotten there, and more probably weren't far behind, he made another break for it. The officer sprinted after him, and we piled into the car, cackling as we sped away.

On a different night about a year later, I was pulled over by the police while driving my friend's car about thirty minutes after leaving a nightclub. I was always the designated driver because I didn't drink (and still don't). For some reason, I vividly remember my dad telling me in elementary school, "If you don't want to break your mom's heart, never drink alcohol and never smoke cigarettes." He probably doesn't even remember saying that, and in retrospect it was likely a little tongue-in-cheek. But for some reason it's always stuck with me.

As I slowly pulled my friend's white, early-nineties Cadillac de Ville into an abandoned parking lot about 2:30 a.m. and multiple police cars pulled in behind us with their blue lights swirling, he looked at me like he'd seen a ghost. "John Wayne's in the trunk," he said quietly, referencing his nickname for the forty-caliber pistol he sometimes stashed under the spare tire.

Jay-Z's "99 Problems" wouldn't come out until the following year, but similar thoughts were running through my mind: "Well, my glove compartment is locked, so is the trunk in the back, and I know my rights so you gon' need a warrant for that."

But as we'd come to find out, a fight had broken out in the nightclub parking lot and someone had pulled a gun and fired a few shots before speeding off in a "white sedan." The police said they had probable cause to search the vehicle; they weren't asking. So the five of us—all basketball players on the local college team—sat separated on a curb watching them rummage through every nook and cranny…except, inexplicably, the compartment under the spare tire. So we all slept in our own dorm rooms that night, instead of at the city jail.

Another disaster averted. And there were many other near misses over the years.

But we wouldn't always be quite so fortunate. When a fight broke out in another nightclub, one of my closest friends growing up—who would later be a groomsman in my wedding—took a bullet in the upper chest and was rushed to the hospital, but survived.

I can't point to a definite, single moment in time when God took the anger out of my heart. But I remember the moment when I fully realized God wasn't just the "clockmaker" in the sky who set the universe in motion but was not actively involved in its events—the moment when I knew that he was actually ordering my steps (Psalm 37:23).

I was playing college basketball at a university in Mississippi, but had decided I wanted to transfer. A friend I grew up with was playing at Enterprise State in tiny Enterprise, Alabama, and he encouraged me to visit. I did, and to my great surprise I actually liked it. So when the coach offered me a scholarship to transfer, I took it.

Meanwhile, on a completely separate track, my family was living in Florida. My dad, who's a Baptist minister, got a call from one of his closest friends, who was a fellow pastor. He said that he would soon be the pastor of Hillcrest Baptist Church... in Enterprise, Alabama...and he asked if my dad would be interested in joining him.

Because of these completely separate events, without any coordination whatsoever, I was reunited with my family in a tiny Alabama town that neither of us had heard of before.

In retrospect, it's hard for me not to get emotional about this moment—one that even the world's most fervent atheist would struggle to chalk up to mere coincidence. Because even at a time when I wasn't particularly concerned with what God's plan was for my life, he was working to bring it to fruition anyway.

My Introduction to Politics

My first time attending church in our new town, I walked into a Sunday school class and was greeted by a man in his late thirties. He was there teaching the college kids. "I like your Mr. T starter kit," he said, nodding at the gold chain around my neck and laughing. I like this guy, I thought, not yet knowing the impact he would end up having on my life.

That man's name was Barry Moore. Today he's more commonly referred to by his title—"congressman." At the time he was an entrepreneur who owned a waste management company. "A garbage man," as he would modestly put it. He and his wife, Heather, had three young kids. And for the first time in my life, I looked up to a man other than my father, and even if I wouldn't say it out loud, I wanted to emulate him.

Starting out, all of us know only the small world that we were born into. I'd never known anyone who'd started and run a successful business. What do people with money do differently than the rest of us? What's going on in the world outside of the deep South? How the heck would I know? I'd never even been on an airplane. What do people talk about if it's not things—or other people? As it turns out, it's ideas—about faith, sure, but also about how to solve tough problems and turn concepts into reality, and about what kind of world we could create and what type of government we should live under. And politics. Oh yes, politics.

When Barry decided to run for the state legislature in 2010, he said to me, "I've never done this. And I know you've never done this either. But I'm betting we can figure it out." Between Barry, his wife, me, and a small team, we did. Through that process, I was bitten by the political bug. And six years after that first successful campaign, I had an office in the West Wing.

A lot happened in between, and not just professionally. Over time, God transformed almost everything about me. At one point a friend I grew up with joked that he couldn't remember the last time he'd heard me curse. "Those political people polished you up," he said derisively.

I hadn't even thought about it, but if my friend had spent any time with "political people," he would have known they definitely weren't the ones cleaning up my language. As Matthew 12:34 says, "out of the abundance of the heart the mouth speaks," and so even though "no human being can tame the tongue" (James 3:8), my heart was being filled with different things, and the words coming out of my mouth started reflecting that.

My life was becoming a different type of fight, one that John Piper summed up better than I ever could:

There is a mean, violent streak in the true Christian life.
But violence against whom, or what? Not other people.

It's a violence against all the impulses in us that would be violent to other people. It's a violence against all the impulses in our own selves that would make peace with our own sin and settle in with a peacetime mentality. It's a violence against all lust in ourselves, and enslaving desires for food or alcohol or pornography or money or the praise of men, and the approval of others or power or fame. It's violence against the impulses in our own soul toward racism and sluggish indifference to injustice and poverty and abortion. Christianity is not a settle-in-and-live-at-peace-with-this-world-the-way-it-is kind of religion. Christianity is war—on our own sinful impulses.

That war wages inside of me to this day, and I hope it continues until the day I die. And when I'm standing face-to-face with the One who won the war against sin for all of eternity, I hope I can echo Paul's words in 2 Timothy 4:7, "I have fought the good fight, I have finished the race, I have kept the faith," and I trust I will hear the response that will make it all worth it: "Well done, good and faithful servant" (Matthew 25:21).

But until then, I still sometimes feel stuck between two worlds. Such is the nature of the widening socioeconomic divide in America. As Thomas Jefferson wrote to John Adams late in life, reflecting on the divisions of their own era, "Every one takes his side in favor of the many, or of the few."

I come from the many, and I've lived and worked among the few.

I love the sense of community, grit, and toughness of the lower-class neighborhoods where I spent so much time growing up. And my imagination is sparked by the whole-world-is-at-my-fingertips thinking of the billionaires, world leaders, and global movers and shakers I've come to know in my thirties. But in both worlds, there's a sense in which I'm now on the outside looking in. The band the Postal Service captured it in a line from their song about Washington, D.C., "I am a visitor here; I am not permanent."

What I'm talking about now, though, is deeper than socioeconomics or culture or lived experience. It's more visceral than politics. It's the reality of what Christians have always endured and will always endure in ways both subtle and aggressive, veiled and overt, when the world makes good on Jesus' promise to his apostles: "you will be hated by all for my name's sake" (Matthew 10:22). Because "if you were of the world, the world would love you as its own; but because you are not of the world, but I chose you out of the world, therefore the world hates you" (John 15:19).

Unfortunately, some elements—perhaps even the most popular elements—of the American church have watered down the truth of the Christian life to the point that it barely resembles what we read in the New Testament.

John the Baptist was beheaded (Matthew 14). James was executed by sword (Acts 12). Stephen was stoned to death—and not on the orders of a tyrant, but by the religious establishment (Acts 7). Stephen's story in particular has always stuck with me because as he was being stoned, he said, "Behold, I see the heavens opened, and the Son of Man standing at the right hand of God" (Acts 7:56).

In Matthew 26, Mark 14, and Luke 22, Jesus tells the High Priest, "You will see the Son of Man seated at the right hand of God." This visual is commonplace in the Bible, and this language is frequently used in the church: God reigns in heaven and Jesus is seated at his right hand. But in this one—and only one—instance in scripture, Jesus is not sitting beside the Father; he's standing.

Surely this isn't a coincidence, right? That in this one moment, when Stephen's boldness in sharing the Gospel is costing him his life, Jesus rises out of his throne. Why? Perhaps Acts 7:59 gives us an indication. "And as they were stoning Stephen, he called out, 'Lord Jesus, receive my spirit.'"

Jesus stood to receive Stephen. Because our God is the God of the outcasts. The prostitutes and prodigals, the lepers, the sick and crippled, the orphans and widows, the working man and the powerless. "The least of these" (Matthew 25:40).

America hungers for this Gospel. Not the soft, timid, feel-good, watered-down version. The real deal. Don't believe me? Let's return to Stephen's story.

"Then they cast him out of the city and stoned him. And the witnesses laid down their garments at the feet of a young man named Saul…And falling to his knees [Stephen] cried out with a loud voice, 'Lord, do not hold this sin against them'" (Acts 7:58, 60).

This Saul, the man who "approved of [Stephen's] execution" (Acts 8:1), would become Paul, the apostle and most prolific author in the New Testament. But first, he saw the Christians he was persecuting—even to death—willing to give it all so that even a man like him could come to Jesus.

What an opportunity for all of us outcasts.

CHAPTER 1

The Wilderness: Anxiety, Uncertainty, & God's Plan

A re you willing to keep running, even when the distance is unknown?

Life is what's known as an infinite game. Finite games are familiar to us all. Every sport or board game has defined rules, a certain number of players, and a clear beginning and end. The goal is to win, and so by definition there is also a loser, at which point the game is over.

Infinite games are different. The purpose is not to win, but to continue playing. Wars, for instance, are finite games, but geopolitics is infinite. Likewise, each of our earthly lives is finite, with a clear beginning and end. But life itself is infinite. There is constant change, and different players—some of whom we know, most of whom we don't—have different goals and different ideas of what success looks like. And the game just rolls on. After all, there's no definitive "winner" of this game called life.

Unfortunately, most of us spend our lives trapped—usually unknowingly—in a finite mindset, as if we're playing a typical game. So we burn out, get discouraged, feel hopeless—and, tragically, some quit. To be sure, there can be finite games inside of an infinite game. Your company can win or lose a pitch for a new client, but there is no definitive winner of the game of "business." A political candidate can win an election, but there is no definitive winner of "politics." Similarly, we can win or lose a momentary battle with sin, but we are freed from the burden of overcoming sin alone, because someone else won that game on our behalf.

So our spiritual journey is an infinite game. There are peaks and valleys, times of close fellowship and periods of solitude in the wilderness—each of an unknowable length and intensity.

So again, I ask, are you willing to keep running, even when the distance is unknown?

Doomsday

What happens in the event of a nuclear attack? What if a category 5 hurricane devastates a major American city to the point of paralysis? What if an electromagnetic pulse (EMP) attack takes the power grid offline, decimates communications networks and GPS, indefinitely pauses critical services, and causes widespread civil unrest?

If you have ever watched one of Hollywood's many doomsday blockbusters, you have asked yourself these questions. You also probably hoped that someone out there has already thought through these potential real-life disasters and come up with a plan.

There are, in fact, plans for ensuring continuity of government (COG) in the event of a catastrophe. However, some of these plans are so secret that a former White House chief of staff once described being transported to a COG site with his eyes and ears covered on the way so that he still would not know where he was located once he got there.

One winter day during my time in government, I joined other top intelligence officials hundreds of feet underground in one of these top-secret facilities discussing the government's continuity of operations plan (COOP). I have to admit, it felt a lot like the movies. A metal blast door several feet thick opened to reveal an enormous tunnel leading to an underground city. A thin layer of moisture coated some of the tunnel walls, the result of rainwater trickling down through the rock from many stories above. There was an eerie stillness in the cool, damp air, broken only by the whir of golf carts moving us from one area to the next. Once inside the operations center, we found staff monitoring giant video screens 24/7; and everything the government would need to continue functioning—or to respond to an attack—was at our fingertips. We inspected sleeping quarters and ate lunch in what must be the world's most heavily fortified cafeteria, which included a made-to-order grill.

This was doomsday prepping on a whole other level—a surreal experience.

I could not help but wonder what life must be like for the people who work in the facility every day. How could you function while spending all your time contemplating our impending doom? How could anyone work in that environment and still heed the Bible's instructions in Matthew 6:34 to "not be anxious about tomorrow, for tomorrow will be anxious for itself"?

You don't have to work in a top-secret nuclear bunker to struggle with anxiety, or even to fear that our world is collapsing. In fact, a recent study revealed that 83 percent of Americans are stressed out and worried about the future.[1] We have become a nation—and more sadly, a church—of worriers. So how should we live in a time of chaos, division, and uncertainty?

The Bible makes it clear that faith and preparedness are not contradictory. Hebrews 11:7 says, "in faith Noah...constructed an ark for the saving of his household." In Genesis 41, Joseph stored up grain during bountiful years so that the people would not starve when a famine came. Even God planned ahead for our coming Savior. When the angel foretold the birth of John the Baptist, he said John would come "to make ready for the Lord a people prepared" (Luke 1:17).

Prepare for the future, but do so with total faith in God's sovereignty, remembering Proverbs 16:9, "The heart of man plans his way, but the Lord establishes his steps." Our God is in control.

Ultimately our worry is often a symptom of a deeper problem: a lack of faith. In Mark 9, when a man brought his son to

Jesus for healing, Jesus said to him, "All things are possible for one who believes," to which the man responded with a simple but perfect prayer for us today: "I believe; help my unbelief" (Mark 9:24)!

The Need to Know

"So, what about UFOs? Are there aliens in Area 51?" Since leaving the intelligence community, I have been asked some variation of these questions more than any others—by far.

Inside the government, they aren't called UFOs. They're commonly referred to as UAPs, unidentified anomalous phenomena. It doesn't require a security clearance to know that there have been some eyebrow-raising things happening in the skies over our country from time to time.

Former Director of National Intelligence John Ratcliffe, who was the country's "top spy" and my direct boss, noted on Fox News that "there are a lot more sightings than have been made public...We are talking about objects that have been seen by Navy or Air Force pilots, or have been picked up by satellite imagery, that frankly engage in actions that are difficult to explain—movements that are hard to replicate that we don't have the technology for, or traveling at speeds that exceed the sound barrier without a sonic boom."[2]

Are these alien spacecraft? Have the Chinese or Russians made some kind of technological leap that we're not aware of and now far exceed our own capabilities? Are these actually

American aircraft that are just so secret that even senior officials don't know they exist? Like anybody, we wanted to know the answers to these questions when we came into office.

The day the government officials who work on such programs showed up to deliver a classified briefing, something interesting happened. They refused to talk in front of the group of senior officials who normally were in the room for such briefings, all of whom had the highest security clearances in the U.S. government. They politely but firmly asked that most people be kicked out of the room. Again, this included even some of the people who viewed basically every bit of classified information that flowed into the Office of the Director of National Intelligence.

That's about all I can say about that.

Need-to-know (NTK) is a foundational concept inside the intelligence community. Just because you have the requisite security clearance needed to view information doesn't mean that you will actually have access to it. You don't get to just browse through classified information for the fun of it. Highly sensitive intelligence is restricted to only the people who need to know it to perform the duties of their jobs.

It can sometimes feel like God has us on the strictest NTK protocols, not just with respect to global and national events but in our day-to-day lives. Why did [insert seemingly terrible thing] happen to me? Why have you put me in this situation? What is God's will? The answers to these questions can feel elusive. There are many mysteries of God's design and in the way he works. There's the conflict between God's foreknowledge and man's exercise of free will, the inability of our finite minds to fathom eternity, and the question of how an all-knowing God can choose to forget our sins against him—just to name a few.

As Christians, our relationship to God is sort of like our relationship to outer space. We know space is out there—we see the stars and planets. But humans have only explored a tiny fraction of the universe. The vast majority of its galaxies remain uncharted; most of its secrets remain unknown.

If we're being honest with ourselves, the incessant impulse to figure things out in our own lives often comes from our desire to be self-reliant, to maintain the illusion of control over our circumstances. We basically want a crystal ball.

The extraordinary gift of the Gospel is that we can know the God of the universe. And what's even more mind-blowing is that he knows us and desires a relationship with us. But we will never fully know him in this life. "For my thoughts are not your thoughts, neither are your ways my ways, declares the Lord. For as the heavens are higher than the earth, so are my ways higher than your ways and my thoughts than your thoughts," says Isaiah 55:8–9. That may be frustrating at first read, but if it weren't true, what kind of God would he be? Would you really want the entire universe—not to mention your own life—to depend on a being whose abilities, thoughts, and ways were fully understandable by our tiny, fallible minds?

"The secret things belong to the Lord our God, but the things that are revealed belong to us and to our children forever, that we may do all the words of this law," says Moses in Deuteronomy 29:29. In other words, God has chosen not to reveal some things to us. But that's okay because he has given us his Word, the most incredible guide for our lives that we could ever hope for. We have carte blanche clearance to peruse the divinely inspired words of God. The Bible lays out his will for what he commands us to do, and we have faith that even though the mysteries of his future plans are strictly NTK and we're not on the clearance list, he's working everything together for our good and for his glory (Romans 8:28).

Paul David Tripp puts it like this: "He tells you the things you need to know to live as you were designed to live, and then he graces you with his presence and his power."[3]

I Make People Disappear for a Living

In the early days of my time working in the intelligence community, I just wanted to soak it all in. I sat quietly in most meetings of the nation's most senior intelligence officials and tried to make sense of the alphabet soup of acronyms they used for everything. I read in-depth reports analyzing intelligence collected in every corner of the world, familiarizing myself with the nuances of high-priority regions and intelligence domains. For anyone who's fascinated by world events and has a hunger for learning, there's not much more stimulating than a senior intelligence job.

Before long, I felt like I had found my bearings. The reality is "governing" isn't some kind of superhuman skill that mere mortals could never understand, although a lot of people in Washington would like everyone to think that it is. It's both terrifying and liberating to realize that, as Apple founder Steve Jobs once said, "Everything around you that you call life was made up by people that were no smarter than you."[4] Or at least that's how I was feeling a few weeks into my tenure in the Office of the Director of National Intelligence.

One afternoon I was standing in a sensitive compart-mented information facility (SCIF) where some of the nation's most sensitive intelligence meetings took place. Secure video teleconference (SVTC) equipment was hanging on the wall, connecting us to high-ranking national security officials from around the U.S. government. The conversation was moving briskly, as it always did, and I suddenly felt confident that I had something of value to add to the discussion. As one of my colleagues finished his thought—or seemed like he had—I interjected. I don't remember what I said, but everyone's head swung in my direction, and he cut his eyes at me and dead-panned: "I make people disappear for a living. Why would you ever interrupt me?"

There was a millisecond of silence in which I considered the accuracy of this comment. I knew what this guy did. I was familiar with his résumé. And while he didn't exactly "make people disappear for a living," the sentiment was close enough to reality that I decided I probably wouldn't interrupt him again anytime soon. Then he burst out laughing, and everyone in the room breathed a sigh of relief.

Have you ever spent time around someone so anxious to show off their knowledge that they couldn't let you finish a sentence before interjecting in order to get to your point faster than you or, worse, to shut down the conversation? I've been around people like that at times, and at other times I'm pretty sure I've been that person.

Now imagine for a second that you actually do know everything there is to know about a given subject. Actually, imagine that you know everything there is to know about literally every subject. But when you try to speak, someone interrupts you, or insists that they've got a better plan, or just ignores you altogether, as if you don't exist.

What arrogance it must take for us to constantly supplant the will of the One who, as the prophet Daniel wrote, "changes times and seasons...removes kings and sets up kings" (Daniel 2:21)! Ego is a heck of a drug. The only way to start fighting this destructive pride—which at its essence is seeking satisfaction in ourselves rather than in God—is to give God the credit that he deserves, both in our hearts and with our mouths. Salvation itself begins with the Father drawing us in (John 6:44), and is entirely made possible by the sacrifice Jesus made on the cross (Ephesians 2:9). He orders all of our steps (Psalm 37:23), and apart from him we can do nothing (John 15:5).

By consistently acknowledging these truths, our egos will be less of a barrier to Christ accomplishing his purposes through us, because "God opposes the proud but gives grace to the humble" (James 4:6). And after all, God makes the entire universe work together, from the tiniest quarks to the largest supermassive black hole. So why would we ever interrupt him?

The Apostle Paul said it best:

Consider your calling, brothers: not many of you were wise according to worldly standards, not many were powerful, not many were of noble birth. But God chose what is foolish in the world to shame the wise; God chose what is weak in the world to shame the strong; God chose what is low and despised in the world, even things that are not, to bring to nothing things that are, so that no human being might boast in the presence of God. And because of him you are in Christ Jesus, who became to us wisdom from God, righteousness and sanctification and redemption, so that, as it is written, "Let the one who boasts, boast in the Lord." (1 Corinthians 1:26–31)

Dreams in the White House

I can't imagine what it must be like to actually live in the White House. As the First Family, you're surrounded by historical artifacts and almost completely confined inside a menagerie in which you are the living centerpiece. It's like *Night at the Museum* meets *The Truman Show*.

While the West Wing is cramped and sometimes underwhelming to first-time visitors, the executive residence is much larger than it appears from the outside. The rooms are spacious and masterfully decorated, seamlessly combining modern luxury with historic charm.

But of all of the residence's grandeur, the coolest feature to me was the family theater. It's not the swankiest. In fact, the red velvet seats are fairly worn and probably haven't been updated in decades. But they're worn in the same way your favorite college sweatshirt is worn—just right, cozy, and comfortable.

President Trump would occasionally invite senior aides and their family members to join him for a movie night. My wife, Megan, is pretty unimpressed by most "perks" of being around politicians, but getting invited to the family theater in the White House was a notable exception. The first movie the president invited us to watch was *La La Land* starring Ryan Gosling as a struggling musician and Emma Stone as an aspiring actress. We entered the East Wing and walked halfway up the East Colonnade, and the White House ushers had popcorn and drinks set out on a table just outside the theater doors.

It was best to get there early and sit down in the second row, just behind the four oversized lounge chairs reserved for the First Family. That way you'd get a running commentary from the president throughout the movie, which was usually pretty hilarious.

"Wow, now here's a good-looking group," Trump said as he walked in. He was in a good mood. "All right, let's get going. I hear it's a good one, but we'll see. You never know."

With everyone settled, the residence staff closed a curtain in front of the double doors where we had entered, encasing the entire theater in dark red fabric. The projector cranked up, piercing the darkness with colorful light, and the movie began to play.

It became obvious pretty quickly that Trump was liking this one. He would subtly nod his head in rhythm during musical numbers, or tap his foot, or his finger on the arm of the chair. He laughed as Ryan Gosling's character refused to play Christmas songs, in spite of his boss's orders, opting for jazz numbers instead. He talked very little during the movie, only occasionally leaning over to say things like "great song" or "she can really dance." He watched intently as both of the lead characters wrestled with the tension between chasing their dreams and pursuing their love for each other.

This was the central plotline of the movie, and as we watched I thought back to the journey Megan and I had been on over the last decade.

The first time we saw each other, I was playing basketball in college. Then for the first several years of our relationship I was a professional musician, touring around the country playing in a large venue or arena one week and small clubs the next. Sometimes we'd share the stage with chart-topping bands and gather around televisions to hear our songs on MTV; other times we'd be on tour in a van for months playing with indie bands in front of tiny crowds. Then I decided to return to college to finish my degree. Then I built a media company. Then I went to work on a presidential campaign that everyone thought was doomed. Now there was only one room between my office and the Oval Office, and we were watching movies with the president of the United States. Later I would become an author and then the CEO of an ad agency, before returning to government in the Office of the Director of National Intelligence.

That's more plot twists than could fit into any plausible movie script. But it also disproved the implied premise of *La La Land*: that love for and commitment to another person precludes the possibility of pursuing big dreams together. But what does the Bible say about chasing dreams anyway? I have to admit that I didn't ask myself this question early enough or often enough. Over the years, I've been much more likely to ask God to help me reach my dreams than to spend time exploring whether I should be pursuing them at all.

Jesus said, "If anyone would come after me, let him deny himself and take up his cross and follow me" (Matthew 16:24). That verse suggests that there are at least some aspects of ourselves—desires we have, things we want to pursue in life—that we must deny. So just because we want to do something doesn't mean that we should.

We also see Paul in Romans 12 saying that God, by his grace, has given us all different gifts—and that we should use them! And so we shouldn't let a misguided attempt at self-sacrifice prevent us from using our talents and passions.

So how do we figure out which dreams to chase and which ones to abandon, or perhaps leave for another time?

We often spend a lot of time focused on our actions; we want to "do" the right thing, "be" better. This is a positive sentiment, but focusing on our actions will never work because our actions are just an outward reflection of our thinking. This is why Paul urges us to "set your mind on things that are above, not on things that are on earth" (Colossians 3:2) and to "take every thought captive to obey Christ" (2 Corinthians 10:5). In other words, if we're going to pursue the right dreams—the ones that God has for us—we need to think like him; then our actions will follow.

So how does God think? He's given us his Word to reveal his thinking to us as we study and meditate on it. From his Word, we can clearly see that his ultimate design is to make his name more glorified around the world.

As he reveals this truth to us in deeper and deeper ways, it changes the way we think, and transforms the desires of our heart. Is spreading his glory the reason we are pursuing whatever dream has consumed our thinking? His desires become our desires. His dreams become our dreams. And from there, we can pursue them with reckless abandon, holding fast to his promise, "Behold, I am with you always, to the end of the age" (Matthew 28:20).

If we do that, we'll be able to look back on our lives in this world the way Trump reviewed *La La Land* at the end of the night. "Pretty good, right? It was better than I thought it was going to be."

Raiders of the Lost Correspondence

All I could think was that I had just walked into the final scene of *Indiana Jones: Raiders of the Lost Ark*, when the camera slowly zooms out to reveal a football-field–size warehouse where the government had stashed crates full of no-telling-what over the course of decades. But this was real life; and every box, shelf, and container was full of letters and gifts for President Trump sent from Americans from every state and every imaginable walk of life.

There was a giant hammer, perfectly crafted to replicate Thor's hammer from the Marvel comic books and movies. It weighed about thirty pounds and had an American flag carved into one side and "TRUMP" embossed on the other in all caps. Resting on a desk was a wooden carving of the president's hand flashing its usual thumbs-up. As I rummaged through the clutter I found an enormous metal ring, forged with the president's iconic silhouette on its face. Stacked side-by-side on metal shelves were dozens of paintings, including one of the president standing atop the U.S. Capitol, holding a child out above a massive crowd in the same way Rafiki held Simba in *The Lion King*. Draped over chairs were enormous quilts and knitted blankets with "Make America Great Again" stitched into them. Organized and set apart from the clutter were military service medals sent in from war heroes, accompanied by heartfelt letters.

Located on the top floor of the Eisenhower Executive Office Building right next to the West Wing, the Correspondence Office was where all the mail sent to the White House eventually found its way after going through security screenings. I realized that this was a gold mine of letters from everyday Americans, and so I asked the office to regularly pull the most compelling ones for me to be able to share with the president, first lady, or staff who might be in a position to help the senders, or make a dream come true, or just brighten their day.

As I look back now at my time in the White House, nothing warms my heart more than remembering the face of a little girl with a rare brain disease running up to hug the president backstage at the National Prayer Breakfast (more on her later!), or the quivering voice of a military veteran thanking the president for supporting his son who was deployed in Afghanistan, or an entrepreneurial little boy cutting the grass in the Rose Garden as the president applauded in approval, or two little girls baking cookies with the first lady in the White House kitchen.

All of those moments started with a letter to the president that worked its way through the Correspondence Office and eventually landed on my desk in the West Wing.

There were stories behind each of the objects and letters, many of them deeply personal. Some people were asking for help. Others were expressing support, opposition, anger, or appreciation. But they all had one thing in common: They wanted the president of the United States to hear their story, to understand where they were coming from. And every one of them, even the most desperate, was tinged with the hope that someone, maybe even the president, would care.

Prayer can sometimes feel like blindly mailing a letter to the White House. Even if we believe in our hearts that God will hear us, a lingering doubt can creep in. All of us have felt distant from God at one point or another, almost like our prayers are bumping up against the ceiling. Even David seems to have felt that way in Psalm 22: "My God, my God, why have you forsaken me?... I cry by day, but you do not answer, and by night, but I find no rest."

In reality, praying isn't anything like sending a letter to the president and hoping that by some stroke of luck and good fortune he might read it. The Bible is crystal clear: God hears us (1 John 5:14–15). But his silence can sometimes be deafening, even though this is a feature, not a bug, of how he works in our lives.

Right before God appeared to Moses in the burning bush, he had been silent for forty years as Moses wandered the wilderness. Even after Samuel anointed David as the future king, he had to return to the fields to tend the sheep, before later emerging to slay Goliath. After Paul's dramatic encounter with God on the road to Damascus, seventeen years passed (Galatians 1:17–19; Galatians 2:1) before he was sent out from the church at Antioch on the most famous missionary journey of all time (Acts 13).

God's timing and the reasons for his silence are two of the Christian life's great mysteries. But it's during these in-between times and periods of silence that he humbles us, purifies our hearts, and strengthens our faith in preparation for what is to come.

Gain hope and assurance during these seasons through the Lord's words to the people of Israel (who would soon be in exile for seventy years) through his prophet Jeremiah: "I know the plans I have for you... Plans for welfare and not for evil, to give you a future and a hope. Then you will call upon me and come and pray to me, and I will hear you. You will seek me and find me, when you seek me with all your heart" (Jeremiah 29:11–13).

Fully Present on Air Force One

The first time I ever traveled with the president, I started out in a column of blacked-out government vans flying down the highway to Joint Base Andrews, where Air Force One was idling. Our vans pulled right up to the iconic plane shimmering in the morning sunlight. Stewards had placed at each seat a quarter-page-size piece of paper adorned with the Presidential Seal and bearing a name to mark where each passenger should sit. In the staff cabin, large leather seats faced each other with a table between them. Food and beverage menus were folded on each table, and I immediately placed an order even though I had too many butterflies in my stomach to actually be hungry.

The moment the president boarded the plane, we took off and made the half-hour flight to Langley Air Force Base in Hampton, Virginia. When we landed, the president disembarked and immediately boarded Marine One, while the rest of us ran up the open bay doors of an Osprey, a hybrid helicopter-airplane. Once buckled in, we choppered five minutes and landed on the deck of the world's largest aircraft carrier, the USS *Gerald R. Ford*, where the President was set to deliver remarks. After assembling our group on the flight deck, a basketball-court–size elevator—typically used for aircraft—lowered us down into the hangar bay. As soon as the president was visible, the thousands of sailors waiting below erupted in deafening applause as we descended. It was like a WWE entrance. Once he finished his remarks, we reversed the process—up the giant elevator, Osprey to Langley, Air Force One to Andrews, blacked-out vans to the West Wing.

When I think back on that day, I feel like I can remember every detail: the HMX-1 insignia on the Marine helicopter, signifying they were the squadron tasked with transporting the president and his team; the president's green bomber jacket, one of the few times other than on the golf course when I saw him without a suit coat; the sound of my grandfather's voice when the operator told him he had a call from Air Force One. It was one of the few days in my life when I was completely and fully present. I wasn't checking my phone or the news. I wasn't daydreaming about or dreading some future event, or reminiscing about or regretting something in the past. Unfortunately it often feels impossible to be present.

Very few things are a greater barrier to hearing God, or consistently living at the center of his will, than our minds constantly wandering to some other time and space rather than living in the present moment. We've got to constantly remind ourselves that God not only directs what happens, he also directs when things happen. That truth can change everything about the way we go through our days. Because if "we know that for those who love God all things work together for good, for those who are called according to his purpose" (Romans 8:28), and believe that he makes "everything beautiful in its time" (Ecclesiastes 3:11), then we can live entirely in this moment—and every moment—that God has divinely appointed.

As always, Jesus modeled this better than anyone. When the time had come for him to be betrayed and crucified, Luke 22:44 describes him as "being in agony" as he prayed, to the point that "his sweat became like great drops of blood falling down to the ground." And yet, just days before, he had triumphantly entered Jerusalem and was greeted by a jubilant crowd, chanting "Hosanna in the highest!" It's mind-boggling that Jesus was able to celebrate and enjoy the fulfillment of the prophecy that our King would come "humble, and mounted on a donkey" (Zechariah 9:9), knowing full well that he would soon be betrayed and die an excruciating death on a cross.

Jesus made the most of every moment, in total peace, recognizing that God's timing is perfect. Fortunately, that's made possible for us too, through Jesus' promise to each of us in John 14:27: "My peace I give to you."

Be fully present in every moment today, through the power of God's supernatural peace, and watch how he's able to use even the most routine moments for your good and his glory.

The View from the CIA Seal

On January 20, 2021, at the moment Joe Biden was being inaugurated as the forty-sixth president of the United States, I was standing beside the CIA seal etched into the floor of the agency's headquarters in Langley, Virginia. I stood with my hands in the pockets of my hoodie, shifting my weight back and forth as if I wanted to leave my own imprint on the hallowed ground.

I walked over to my right to see the memorial wall where 135 black stars are chiseled into the white marble to honor CIA officers who gave their lives in service to their country. Many of the stars represent individuals whose names remain classified. But as I looked down at the open Book of Honor, I noticed Johnny Micheal "Mike" Spann, a fellow Alabamian who was the first American killed in Afghanistan at the beginning of the Global War on Terror.

Down the hall I walked slowly by the portraits of every president since the CIA's inception. Each painting is accompanied by a handwritten note hanging underneath, thanking the CIA for its contributions to keeping the country safe, starting with President Truman, who praised them "from someone who knows" the immense value of their work and ending with President Trump, who wrote in all caps how "proud" he was of them. At the end of the corridor I stopped in front of the charred remains of an American flag that was recovered from the rubble of the Twin Towers after 9/11.

Around the corner, two CIA officers were staring up at a TV hanging from the ceiling, watching the inaugural proceedings in silence. It was a transition moment for our country, and I was wandering the nearly empty hallways by myself because I knew it was a transition moment for me as well. A season of my life was coming to a close.

We are creatures of habit. There isn't much we dislike more than a change in our routine. But there is also nothing in life so certain as, well, change. Politics and culture change. People come in and out of our lives. We lose or change jobs. We move. Our children grow up. Our bodies fail us. No matter what is happening in your life right now, things are changing. Sometimes we wake up to a dramatically different life than the one we fell asleep with just hours before.

Ecclesiastes 3 reminds us that "for everything there is a season…a time to be born, and a time to die…a time to weep, and a time to laugh; a time to mourn, and a time to dance…a time to keep silence, and a time to speak…a time for war, and a time for peace." But the ultimate reassurance throughout every season of life is found in Malachi 3:6: "For I the Lord do not change."

On top of that, our unchanging God actually cares about the twists and turns of our lives. Even just hours before he was to be executed, Jesus' heart was burdened for his disciples. "Peace I leave with you; my peace I give to you," Jesus told them. "Let not your hearts be troubled, neither let them be afraid" (John 14:27).

No matter what changes come our way, we have an unchanging, unfailing God who is not just along for the ride; he is working all things together for our good and for his glory (Romans 8:28). Pray for God to give you his peace in the midst of uncertainty.

CHAPTER 2

The Way: Work, Culture Wars,
& Counting the Cost

"How much do you think that bird's worth?"

The forty-person White House communications team was huddled together in the Roosevelt Room late in the afternoon, and I was listening to a small group of junior aides debate the cost of a golden eagle statue in the corner of the room. The sculptures—there were actually two of them, one on each side of a large cabinet that hid a giant flat-screen TV behind its antique doors—stood about two feet tall. They had been added to the room as part of the latest round of renovations.

The eagles were each perched atop a rock with their wings extended high above their heads, like they were stuck on the first letter of the "YMCA" dance.

"Gotta be, like, twenty thousand dollars, or something like that," one of the young aides estimated.

"I'm pretty sure it's bronze, not gold," argued another. "Probably knock it down some. I'd guess ten thousand."

"What's up with certain parts looking darker than others, though?" a third chimed in.

"It's called patina, dude," the second one shot back incredulously.

I chuckled to myself as they walked across the room together to get a closer look. I already knew what they were about to find out: the eagles were actually made of wood, not some precious metal. The statues were intricately carved and beautifully painted. But they weren't quite what my colleagues thought they were going to be.

That story isn't a perfect metaphor for the attraction of power, but I do vividly recall the cognitive dissonance of finally sitting in my West Wing office. I had once stood on Pennsylvania Avenue and wondered what must be happening behind those white walls and curtained windows. Actually working in the office, though, wasn't what it seemed to be from the outside looking in. And while I learned in the process that I was much more susceptible to the allure of power than I had previously known, I also learned that the attainment of power would never fulfill me.

And yet, somehow, it's still hard to resist.

But if power is alluring—and it is!—persecution, on the other hand, strikes me as something to avoid like the plague. Why have a conversation about the Gospel with a friend or colleague when it could result in rejection and the loss of social status? Why not just go with the flow when doing otherwise could make me a pariah? Or perhaps more specifically, why write a book about faith lessons from the halls of power, when I might one day be sitting in a confirmation hearing and have a senator suggest that my faith would have too great an influence on my decision-making, like when Senator Dianne Feinstein derisively told Supreme Court nominee Amy Coney Barrett, "The dogma lives loudly within you"?

This chapter is an exploration of what it takes to prepare for being entrusted by God with either power or persecution—and perhaps both at different times, or even simultaneously. It's also a window into my own wrestling with a reality that every Christian in America has to be prepared to face: being outspoken about our faith and fully adhering to our beliefs might actually cost us something, especially professionally.

"I know how to be brought low, and I know how to abound. In any and every circumstance, I have learned the secret of facing plenty and hunger, abundance and need. I can do all things through him who strengthens me" (Philippians 4:11–13).

The Nuclear Football

Standing in the West Wing one afternoon, I struck up a conversation with President Trump's military aide. "Let me hold that thing," I joked, pointing down at the president's emergency satchel (more commonly referred to as "the nuclear football") sitting at his feet. The Smithsonian called it "the clos-est modern-day equivalent of the medieval crown and scepter—a symbol of supreme authority. Accompanying the commander in chief wherever he goes, the innocuous-looking briefcase is touted in movies and spy novels as the ultimate power accessory, a doomsday machine that could destroy the entire world."[1]

To my surprise, the aide said, "Go ahead," and for the five seconds I held the forty-five-pound bag I felt like I had gained possession of a magical ring out of a J. R. R. Tolkien novel.

Now, before you get worried that I momentarily held the fate of the world in my hands, you have to understand that there is not a giant red button inside the bag that launches missiles. The real purpose of the briefcase's contents is to verify the pres-ident's identity (he carries a card called "the biscuit" with him everywhere he goes that includes identification codes). From there, communications would be opened up with the National Military Command Center in the Pentagon and a menu of pre-planned strike options would be available for review. So rest easy: I wasn't in a position to inadvertently start a nuclear war.

But the nuclear football, a physical manifestation of the incredible power of the presidency, is a reminder of the mag-netic attraction that power has on us all. Being at the center of human power every day in the White House sometimes warped my moral compass. As the nineteenth-century orator Robert G. Ingersoll said, reflecting on the legacy of Abraham Lincoln, "Most people can bear adversity. But if you wish to know what a man really is, give him power. This is the supreme test."[2]

Power dynamics are a part of all of our lives—in our workplaces, in our friend groups, in our churches, and even in our own homes. In any leadership role—from company executives and pastors to parents and Sunday school teachers—we have power and influence over those who follow us. God wants to use for his glory the people he places in positions of power and authority. But we must remember that power is deceptive. It leads us to believe that it is our own. In reality, though, all power is God's. As John Piper put it, "the reason we abuse power is because we do not humbly delight in the glory of God's right to all power. When we are blind to the glory of God's passion to be known and loved as the source and sum of all power, we take it for our own and use it for ourselves."[3]

The way to break free from the bondage that awaits us in the pursuit of power is to find our satisfaction in God. Praise him for the sustaining power he has in your life today, and pray that he will guide you as you seek to use the power he has lent you to accomplish his purpose.

The Most Humble Champion

Days when championship sports teams visited the White House felt like in-office holidays. The mood was upbeat, and people were relaxed.

When the Super Bowl–winning New England Patriots visited us, tight end Rob Gronkowski actually interrupted the daily televised press briefing by poking his head in and asking the press secretary, "Need some help?" All in good fun.

President Trump typically acted as host and tour guide, unable to resist the urge to show everyone around. "You guys want to see the Oval Office?" he asked the World Series–winning Chicago Cubs before piling in the entire team. The Boston Red Sox even got a trip upstairs to the White House residence to see the Lincoln Bedroom.

"You're not supposed to be showing it," Trump joked in front of the cameras. "So if the media doesn't report me for this, I'm going to go up and show them the Lincoln Bedroom. They wanted to see the Lincoln Bedroom so I'll give the tour myself."

When the National Championship–winning football team from my alma mater, the University of Alabama, announced they were coming, it was the only time I explicitly asked to draft the president's remarks. I probably spent more time per word on those remarks than anything else I ever wrote.

Knowing about quarterback Tua Tagovailoa's outspoken Christian faith, I took him into the State Dining Room and showed him John Adams's prayer etched into the white marble mantel:

I Pray Heaven To Bestow The Best Of Blessings On This House And All that shall hereafter Inhabit it. May none but Honest and Wise Men ever rule under This Roof.

In an office that was used to receiving kings and queens, presidents and prime ministers, legendary Alabama coach Nick Saban was still a focus of intense curiosity. The chief of staff of the National Security Council asked him, "What is it that you think has made you so successful? I don't mean this year; I mean year after year after year… What's different about what you do?" You could have heard a pin drop in the Roosevelt Room as we waited intently to hear his answer.

Seeming slightly embarrassed by the attention and praise, Saban politely said, "One thing I learned working for [New England Patriots coach] Bill Belichick is that everyone in an organization has to have clear roles, clear objectives, and they have to be held accountable. It was like that for everyone in the organization, top to bottom—the ball boys to the star quarterback."

But my most memorable experience with a visiting team was actually with Alabama's nemesis, Clemson. I didn't spend much time with them at the White House since they had defeated my Crimson Tide in the National Championship game, but I ran into them at the Capitol, where I had a meeting in the speaker's office later that afternoon.

A massive line formed in the sweltering heat, with everyone waiting to go through security. I was caught in the line, but had a pleasant conversation with a handful of coaches and their families while we waited. I was early for my meeting, and so after making it through the metal detectors, I waited for a House aide who'd escort me to the speaker's office. Meanwhile the massive Clemson entourage kept slowly filing in. About fifteen minutes later, near the end of the line, head coach Dabo Swinney walked in, still wearing his suit but now totally drenched in sweat.

I was stunned. In spite of being the highest-ranking, most important, and most famous person there, he didn't skip the line; he waited in the back. He let almost everyone else go in front of him. I immediately thought about his remarks earlier at the White House, during which he had talked about people focusing on life's big moments while forgetting that, really, life is what happens between those big moments—when character is formed. Coach Swinney's character had already been built to the point that he didn't cut corners in the blistering heat outside the U.S. Capitol, even though he'd already won the National Championship and didn't have anything left to prove.

What a picture of selfless servanthood and humility, especially in a culture obsessed with power and success. John Piper rightly said, "Every good thing in the Christian life grows in the soil of humility."

And in Philippians 2:3–8, the Apostle Paul writes:

Do nothing from rivalry or conceit, but in humility count others more significant than yourselves. Let each of you look not only to his own interests, but also to the interests of others. Have this mind among yourselves, which is yours in Christ Jesus, who, though he was in the form of God, did not count equality with God a thing to be grasped, but made himself nothing, taking the form of a servant, being born in the likeness of men. And being found in human form, he humbled himself by becoming obedient to the point of death, even death on a cross.

The Search for Meaning

There are people in the United States government who know the exact shape and size of certain foreign leaders' ears. If that seems strange, you need a greater appreciation for just how closely we observe every move and listen to every utterance of certain heads of state, particularly those from "hard-target" countries. Using every available means of collecting information—from open-source intelligence like television appearances or newspaper articles, to highly classified intelligence collected from individuals with access, satellite images, or audio intercepts—the U.S. government builds medical and psychological profiles on numerous leaders around the globe. And the intelligence services of other countries work to do the same on the U.S. president and other key officials in our government.

In a report by Dr. Jonathan Clemente, a physician who has written extensively about the secretive medical intelligence unit inside the CIA, one psychologist who worked in the agency noted that foreign leaders are "fallible and sometimes idiosyncratic," and developing a medical and psychological profile of them "contributes to the overall intelligence assessment of the stability of foreign regimes."[4]

In one historical example from the early 2000s, two separate events had the CIA's medical intelligence unit buzzing about Cuban leader Fidel Castro.[5] The first was when Castro tripped and fell during a memorial service for fellow communist revolutionary Che Guevara. "The basic question to be answered was what precipitated this fall?" Clemente wrote in his report. "Was the floor wet? Was he pushed? Did he have a stroke or heart attack? Does he have vertigo? The leader's long-term ability to govern may be dictated by the nature of the medical event." The second event was a couple of years later when the Cuban government announced that Castro had been hospitalized. "It wasn't long before they [CIA] had their best guess: either a bleeding ulcer or acute diverticulitis, both of them in line with Castro's symptoms—extensive internal hemorrhaging and emergency surgery," reported Clemente.

During my time in the Office of the Director of National Intelligence, the director was kept apprised of the intelligence community's latest assessment of various foreign leaders' health and psychological condition.

The intelligence officers who collect and analyze this intelligence devote their lives to searching for meaning in everything. Could that limp suggest multiple sclerosis? Does the new mole in that photograph indicate melanoma? Does a subtle, new facial asymmetry indicate a stroke? Is there any psychological insight to be gleaned from Vladimir Putin channeling his inner Bond villain at a press conference, saying, "There is no happiness in life, only a mirage of it on the horizon"?[6]

This search for meaning is an inherent part of the human condition. On a more practical level, we constantly watch people's body language and listen to their tone of voice so we can "read between the lines" of what they're saying. And of course there are the existential questions. We wonder why we're alive, or whether there's any purpose to anything we experience, especially all the pain.

Here's what we know for certain: If the Gospel is not true, life is indeed meaningless. Paul speaks to this extensively in 1 Corinthians 15. "If Christ has not been raised, your faith is futile and you are still in your sins...[W]e are of all people most to be pitied...'Let us eat and drink, for tomorrow we die.'"

But Paul closes the chapter by declaring with certainty that "in the Lord your labor is not in vain," because "Christ has been raised from the dead," conquering death so that "in Christ shall all be made alive." This is our ultimate hope, and the place we start to find meaning in life.

Unfortunately many preachers have reduced their message to fortune cookie Christianity, substituting self-help platitudes for the true meaning that can be found in the pages of the Bible they rarely bother to reference.

So what is the meaning of life? I don't presume to fully know the answer to that question, but I believe it starts with knowing God and having a relationship with him. No amount of doing, of achieving, of striving for the things of the world could ever replicate the fulfillment that comes from the search for meaning in the pages of scripture.

With that in mind, are you searching for meaning in the right places?[7]

Oval Office Wallpaper and Ordinary Work

Donald Trump is a builder at heart. Building, renovating, haggling over designs and costs—before politics, that was the world he knew best.

During the 2016 campaign, the first time he visited the "war room" in Trump Tower where most of us worked, he became preoccupied with the renovations that had taken place since he'd last visited the fourteenth floor, just above what was once the set of his top-rated television show, *The Apprentice*. No detail seemed to escape his discerning eye. He tapped his black dress shoes on the new carpet. He ran his hands along the doorframes and inspected the trim.

Traditionally every new president, usually with the help of the first lady, makes cosmetic changes to the Oval Office. So once we were in the White House, Trump personally selected the rug (Reagan era), curtains (gold, of course), couches (Bush 43 era), and perhaps most memorably, the wallpaper.

When the White House called York Wallcoverings in Pennsylvania to tell them the president wanted an order for the Oval Office delivered by seven p.m. that same day, they at first thought it was a prank. Then they panicked. Three years before, they'd stopped making the pattern that Trump had now personally selected. So the good folks at York stopped everything else they were working on, hand-mixed the inks, printed ninety-six double rolls of out-of-stock fabric, and made the two-hour drive to deliver the product, all before dinnertime.

Trump's fascination with architecture and design also came out in random conversations. From the day we arrived in Washington, D.C., the J. Edgar Hoover Building (the FBI's aging headquarters on Pennsylvania Avenue) was a particular focus of his ire. "Honestly, I think it's the ugliest building in the city," he said of the massive concrete structure. The building was like a giant tan blob—the size of a city block—with hundreds of tiny square portals for windows. It was built in an architectural style known as "brutalism," and the name was entirely fitting.

The style and design of public buildings matter. They should inspire, silently call us to something greater than ourselves. I used to write and work for hours inside the extraordinary domed reading room of the Library of Congress, overseen by sixteen bronze statues, including Moses and the Apostle Paul.

But of course there's more to beauty than what's just on the surface. It's deeper than that.

How does Matthew 7 say we should judge a tree? By its fruit. There are inherent "good" and "bad" traits that are immediately recognizable—yes, in people, but also in our physical surroundings. We know them when we see them because it's deeper than a difference in taste. For example, the entire Nazi aesthetic just looked evil, didn't it? A child could have picked them out as the bad guys in the same way they'd recognize the villains in a cartoon. Soviet architecture—geometric forms of drab concrete and harsh steel—reflected their brutal communist ideology. ISIS swept across the Middle East with a black flag that accurately communicated impending violence and repression.

Noble ideas produce beauty. Evil ideas produce ugliness. This isn't true only at a macro, societal level; it's also true in each of our daily lives. What does the work we produce say about our hearts?

God created us to display his glory for the world to see—not so God's glory will somehow increase; he's already supremely glorious—but so that his glory will become more known in the world, so that people will recognize it and praise him (Isaiah 43:21). Our work is an opportunity to display God's glory for the world to see and be drawn to him. The first thing we see God doing in Genesis 1 is creating! And part of his plan for our lives is to reflect his character and image by being mini creators ourselves.

Here's how Alabama pastor Matt Mason put it:

"Mothers are an expression of the nurture of God. Artists and entrepreneurs are an expression of the creativity of God. Executives are an expression of the rule of God. Accountants and administrators are an expression of the order of God. Counselors, therapists and medical workers are an expression of the healing power of God. Educators are an expression of the wisdom and knowledge of God. Baristas are an expression of the God who wakes the dead. Volunteer workers are an expression of the God who said, 'It is better to give than to receive.' Hairdressers and fashion designers are an expression of the beauty of God. Marketers and advertisers are a reflection of the persuasive God. Architects and builders are a reflection of the refuge and shelter of God.

Journalists, writers and storytellers are a reflection of the God who makes every word count and saves his best word for last."

All work is sacred when it's done to the glory of God, no matter if it's in the White House or a coffeehouse. So when we're stuck feeling like we're ordinary people living ordinary lives, it's worth shocking ourselves back into an eternal mindset with the simple truth that there is no such thing as "ordinary" work.

Tyranny over the Mind of Man

"WARNING: RESTRICTED U.S. GOVERNMENT INSTAL-LATION," the red, all-caps lettering read as I turned off of Dolley Madison Boulevard. Driving by that sign is the closest most people will ever get to the CIA's fabled Langley headquarters. The first time you drive past it and slowly roll through the compound's heavily armed gates, it's a surreal experience—like at any moment you're going to be swarmed by officers with guns drawn, barking out orders that you have to leave because you're not supposed to be there.

Once I found a parking spot in the sprawling concrete lot north of the building, I walked through an obscure entrance and scanned my badge while standing inside a plastic tube that felt like something out of an eighties sci-fi flick.

Now inside the bowels of the CIA's Original Headquarters Building, I was confronted with a maze of hallways lined with locked doors and plaques with vague descriptions of what might lie behind them. I finally found a bank of elevators and rode up to the main floor where the wide hallways are lined with a mixture of historical paintings and the type of promotional posters found in many corporate settings.

It didn't take long to see how prevalent the agency's "Diversity and Inclusion" office was in the hallways, touting its various programs and initiatives and proclaiming the importance of each officer's "identity." It doesn't take an ethnic or gender studies major to understand the importance of diversity in the intelligence field. Who's going to have an easier time blending in on the streets of Tehran: an ethnic Persian for whom Farsi is their native language, or someone who looks and talks like me? Or perhaps even more relevant, when you're trying to understand the circumstances surrounding a pandemic outbreak that originated in China, wouldn't it probably help to have virologists who are fluent in Mandarin?

But as I turned the corner to walk into the CIA's cafeteria for the first time, it became clear that the agency's diversity focus had a political angle as well. "TRANS LIVES ARE HUMAN LIVES," the poster read. *Even in here,* I thought to myself, considering how someone had taken time out of their day protecting the security of America from dangerous foreign actors in order to promote the latest iteration of identity politics.

In spite of the Left's insistence that Americans need to "trust the science" on any number of issues, ranging from vaccines to climate change, nothing draws their ire more quickly than when someone asserts the basic tenets of human biology, like the fact that having two X chromosomes makes one a female, while having one X and one Y chromosome makes one a male.

In our culture, there will be consequences for anyone who dissents from the idea that gender is a matter of personal choice rather than biological fact—no matter how respectfully one disagrees, and regardless of whether it is out of religious conviction. There will be pressure to conform, to list your pronouns (in the case of the U.S. State Department, they just put their employees' pronouns in all email headers, whether the employees liked it or not), to share bathrooms and locker rooms with individuals of a different sex, to destroy women's sports. Those who disagree are called "bigots" and are not tolerated; the old adage that "the antidote for bad speech is more good speech" only really works when you have the truth on your side.

So what should Christians think of this? The Biblical truth that "God created us male and female" (Genesis 1:27) is a great place to start. This beautiful reality is echoed throughout scripture, from the description of creation in Genesis 2 to God's vision of man and woman coming together as one flesh in marriage (Genesis 2:24, Matthew 19:5, Mark 10:8, Ephesians 5:31)—all of the Bible's gender discussions take place in a binary framework of man and woman.

But practically, how should Christians engage with transgender co-workers, or how should we respond to various identity politics mandates in the workplace? Should we call transgender co-workers by their birth names and pronouns, or the ones they've chosen? Should we acquiesce to mandates that we include our preferred pronouns in email signatures and company memos? Should we willingly share the bathroom with transgender individuals of the opposite biological sex?

We should always have empathy for those who are hurting or confused. Jesus' ministry is marked by compassion for all of us sinners, capped by the greatest act of selfless love in all of history when he laid down his life to save us all. So it is worth considering what we're willing to do to help our transgender friends find liberation in the realization that our true identity is found in Christ alone.

As a practical matter, I can see a case for names being mostly arbitrary; I've chosen to be called "Cliff" rather than "Clifton," for example. But I generally try to avoid using a name that could be taken as tacit affirmation of the falsehood that gender is "fluid" or can be changed. Pronouns, however, are not arbitrary. Calling a "he" a "she" is, according to science, a lie. And violating the privacy of the opposite sex in bathrooms and locker rooms is unacceptable. So I would oppose—and refuse to comply with—any such mandates on the basis that I will not violate my sincerely held religious beliefs to placate anyone's false opinions.

As Thomas Jefferson once wrote, "I have sworn upon the altar of God eternal hostility against every form of tyranny over the mind of man."

So if you want to be at the forefront of today's counterrevolution, be an unabashed rebel against the Left's tyranny of the mind and assault on human biology: get married, start a family, and refuse to live in fear of the mob.

The Idol of Careers

In early September of 2020, I was waiting for President Trump in the Rose Garden of the White House with about a dozen other people who had played integral roles in the Republican National Convention, for which I had led the messaging and speechwriting.

When the president walked out of the Oval Office to greet us all and take a group picture commemorating the moment, he saw me and suddenly stopped everything. "There he is!" the president said, gesturing toward me. "You know, I sued him—I really did a number on him! But, I brought him back because we always loved him, right? We always loved him."

The president was laughing and so was I, but others in the group were exchanging nervous glances and not sure what to make of it all because they did not know the backstory. Before the memoir of my time in the White House was published, the president was given the false impression that my book would be an attack on him. This set off a brief legal dispute that was resolved after he realized I was not attacking him, and we patched things up.

But before that resolution and my return as one of his top intelligence officials, the climax of our misunderstanding happened live on CNN. In the middle of an interview, the president tweeted that I was a "gofer" who had written "made up stories and fiction." The CNN anchor read the tweet aloud—the first time I had heard it—and asked me to respond in the moment.

"My identity is not wrapped up in being a Trump staffer," I said. "My identity is wrapped up in who I am in my faith…I know who Jesus says I am; [it doesn't] matter to me what Donald Trump or anyone else says that I am."

It was the right answer, and I meant it, but it masked the difficult reality that I have always struggled with giving in to the temptation to idolize my career. The nagging, selfish desire to make a name for myself through my work made it difficult to brush aside any public criticism, especially from the president of the United States.

God created work. I know it is a huge part of his plan for my life and he can be glorified in it and through it. But I don't want to be consumed by it.

To ensure that our jobs fit into God's intended purpose for our lives, the authors of *The Gospel at Work* wrote that we must not "make an idol of work," while also not being "idle in work." It's a challenging balance. If you wake up every morning dreading work, or thinking it doesn't matter, remember that idleness in work is just as out of step with God's plan as idolizing work.

The key to finding the right balance between idleness and idolatry is to remember that, as the authors of *The Gospel at Work* wrote, "no matter what you do, your job has inherent purpose and meaning because you are doing it ultimately for the King. Who you work for is more important than what you do." When you think about it that way, work becomes worship.

Prayerfully consider the words of Paul in Colossians 3:23–24—"Whatever you do, work heartily, as for the Lord and not for men, knowing that from the Lord you will receive the inheritance as your reward. You are serving the Lord Christ."

The Minority View

One of the bravest people I met in the halls of the CIA wasn't a case officer who had worked in some dark corner of the Earth, or run a legendary covert operation overseas, or survived some harrowing near-death experience. Those patriots are at the agency for sure, but this particular guy was a tech genius who sat behind a desk at Langley headquarters and analyzed intelligence collected in cyberspace.

During the lead-up to the 2020 presidential election, foreign countries sought to influence the American political system in various ways. At one point, Director of National Intelligence John Ratcliffe even held a press conference—an unprecedented move by the nation's spy chief—to alert the public to election influence operations being conducted by Iran and Russia.

The intelligence community produced a report after the election detailing all these efforts, but when it came to China, there was disagreement. Some analysts said that China had not sought to influence the 2020 presidential election, and the reasoning they gave was that Beijing didn't think it mattered whether Biden or Trump won because anti-China sentiment was strong in both parties. Other analysts concluded from their assessment that China had indeed taken actions to influence the election to hurt Trump. But to our surprise, when we saw a draft of the report before it became public, my brave friend was the only one left willing to call out China's bad actions. He was the only name listed in the minority view.

An investigation into the creation of the report would later reveal an intense pressure campaign to bully my friend and other analysts into suppressing or changing their views.[8] This included participation by "CIA Management" and other intelligence officials "because they tend to disagree with the [Trump] Administration's policies" and they didn't "want our intelligence used to support those policies." But while others caved, my friend did not. He insisted upon sharing his perspective and would not back down under political pressure.

As Director Ratcliffe wrote in a letter to Congress, "Placing [him] on a metaphorical island by attaching his name alone to the minority view is a testament to both his courage and to the effectiveness of the institutional pressures that have been brought to bear on others who agree with him."

Unfortunately for my friend, after Biden became president—and once Director Ratcliffe and I were gone—he was punished by having election-threat analysis taken out of his portfolio and given to someone else. Eventually he was pushed out of his job altogether. He had risked the professional and social consequences of telling the truth, and he paid a price for it.

In the Old Testament book of Numbers, God instructed Moses to "send men to spy out the land of Canaan, which I am giving to the people of Israel." So Moses sent twelve spies into the Promised Land, a leader from each of the tribes, to see if the people were "strong or weak," if the land was "good or bad," and if the people were living in "camps or strongholds."

After forty days, the spies came back with a report. The land was so good it flowed "with milk and honey," they said. But the cities were "fortified and very large," and the inhabitants were so big that God's people were like "grasshoppers" to them. The people panicked. "Why is the Lord bringing us into this land, to fall by the sword?" they exclaimed. "Our wives and our little ones will become prey. Would it not be better for us to go back to Egypt?"

But two of the spies, Joshua and Caleb, offered a minority view. "If the Lord delights in us, he will bring us into this land and give it to us," they told the people. "Do not rebel against the Lord. And do not fear the people of the land, for they are bread for us. Their protection is removed from them, and the Lord is with us; do not fear them."

If you're familiar with this story, you know that Joshua and Caleb were the only two men alive at that time whom God allowed to enter into the Promised Land. What you may have forgotten is that after they gave their "alternative" intelligence analysis, the people rose up to stone them, and they ended up having to wander with the people in the wilderness for forty years before seeing the fulfillment of God's promise.

Doing the right thing is easy until it might actually cost something. We all too often idolize safety—physically, professionally, and reputationally. But the story of Joshua and Caleb is a story of God's faithfulness to those who do his will even when faced with opposition.

Pray for God to give you the wisdom to discern his will and the strength to stay in the center of it, even when it costs you something and especially when it's difficult. History, as shown in God's word and in each of our own lives, proves that it's worth it.

The Inner Ring

Doors to the major rooms in the West Wing—such as the Oval Office, Cabinet Room, and Roosevelt Room—are all outfitted with sturdy, gold-plated hardware. When the knobs turn there's a loud click, followed by the quiet whoosh of a heavy door swinging smoothly on its gilded hinges. When guests are waiting to see the president, nothing stops their nervous conversations quicker than that click, whoosh.

In a city like Washington, D.C., where power is the ultimate currency, the Oval Office is the inner sanctum—the room where it happens, whatever it is. But just outside of the Oval Office's curved door is another small room, aptly called the Outer Oval. The president's assistants have desks there, within earshot of the president's every need; and it's also where senior aides, cabinet secretaries, and guests gather before hearing that click, whoosh and being ushered in to see the president.

During Trump's early days in the White House I was a communications aide. In the morning I would often be in the Outer Oval before he came down from the residence for his intelligence briefing. The CIA director would often be there, along with the president's intelligence briefer, the vice president, the chief of staff, and sometimes others. When the president would arrive, his senior national security team would go into the room, and the door would be shut behind them, leaving everyone else to only wonder what was being discussed inside.

This sparked in me what would become a familiar feeling for many White House aides—a never-ending desire to be in the room, in the know, and as C. S. Lewis once put it, inside the "inner ring."

The temptation of the inner ring exists all throughout our lives. In school, we might want to be on a certain sports team or just sit at the "cool" table at lunch. In college, maybe it's being accepted into the right sorority or fraternity. In the Trump White House, the official org chart looked like a typical White House, starting with the chief of staff at the top and working down from there. The unofficial, real org chart, however, was basically Trump in the middle and everyone he personally knew connected to him—like a hub and its spokes. The inner ring of the White House was being one of those spokes, and most of us would do whatever it took to be (and remain) one of those spokes.

"Unless you take measures to prevent it," C. S. Lewis said, "this desire is going to be one of the chief motives of your life, from the first day on which you enter your profession until the day when you are too old to care... Of all the passions, the passion for the Inner Ring is most skillful in making a man who is not yet a very bad man do very bad things."[9]

How does this happen, you may ask. It most likely won't be a dramatic moment with "obviously bad men, obviously threatening or bribing." No, it will be much more subtle than that, like a small compromise when someone within the ring you desperately want to enter suggests "'we'—and at the word 'we' you try not to blush for mere pleasure—something 'we always do.'"

In these moments, it is good to be reminded of Luke 16:10: "One who is faithful in a very little is also faithful in much, and one who is dishonest in a very little is also dishonest in much."

Because, as Lewis continues, a person who pursues the inner ring may "end in a crash, a scandal, and penal servitude: it may end in millions, a peerage, and giving prizes at your old school." But either way, "you will be a scoundrel." And even if you succeed in going deeper and deeper, entering one ring after another, it won't ever be enough. "As long as you are governed by that desire you will never get what you want. You are trying to peel an onion: if you succeed there will be nothing left. Until you conquer the fear of being an outsider, an outsider you will remain…The quest of the Inner Ring will break your hearts, unless you break it."

CHAPTER 3

The (Great Com)Mission

"Follow me as I follow Jesus!"

His voice was on the verge of a yell, and there was a big part of me that wished he would pipe down. Barely ten yards away, a small group of men, each wearing a long beard and a dish-dāshah (the long white robe typically worn by Muslim men in the Middle East), were glaring at my Arab friend and me. But as long as they were only staring daggers through us, rather than trying to actually stab them through us, I figured that was a win.

We'll call my friend Ahmed, although by his boldness illustrated above I'm sure he'll cringe at my caution in not revealing his real name, especially since I'm writing this more than 6,000 miles removed from the dangers he faces every day.

Ahmed had once been a Muslim imam who was a chaplain in his country's military. He'd started reading the Bible as a research exercise, but God had a different plan. Through the words on those pages, the Holy Spirit moved in Ahmed's heart, and it wasn't long before he had left behind everything he'd ever known to follow Christ.

Now, years later, as Ahmed and I walked through the streets of a Middle Eastern city where it is technically illegal to encourage Muslims to convert to Christianity, he was joyfully defiant. We were looking for a restaurant with some friends, and I'd asked him how close we were, and with an enormous smile on his face, he seized his opportunity to loudly paraphrase the apostle Paul, "Follow my example, as I follow the example of Christ" (1 Corinthians 11:1—NIV).

Once inside, he was no less boisterous. Every time a waiter would come near our table, he would suddenly start talking even louder about his faith in the hope that someone—anyone!— would ask him to tell them more about this Jesus of his.

When I half-jokingly remarked that he walked around like he had a death wish, one of his friends—a woman whom Ahmed had led to Christ—replied, "The Lord will take each of us in his time. Why would we be afraid to die? It would be an honor to die for him instead of just at the end of life."

Words like that hit differently when they're spoken by people for whom the stakes actually are that high. This was at the height of ISIS's run of terror in the region, when reports of them burning and beheading Christians were plastered across western news networks and social media—before Trump took office and ordered ISIS to be annihilated. On the ground, there was a palpable sense that radical Islamists could be hiding in plain sight among the population, quietly looking for opportunities to snatch a westerner or native Christian.

And yet, Ahmed and his small group of Christian friends could not have been less bothered by this terrifying prospect. Because they were not blinded by our western lens—which too often blurs our vision with obstacles and distractions of comfort and consumerism—risking their lives was business as usual for anyone who'd read Jesus' words in Matthew 24:9: "Then they will deliver you up to tribulation and put you to death, and you will be hated by all nations for my name's sake."

When I got back home to the States, I was reminded of how elusive the search for purpose can be when everything is so comparatively peaceful and trouble-free. Our politics is contentious, and Christians in America face tremendous opposition, but our lives aren't at risk like Ahmed's is. Yet in this midst of our safe and comfortable lives, we long for purpose and meaning. Feeling this tension after I returned home made me want to go back, but why?

Fulfillment comes from accomplishing hard things. As the old saying goes, nothing good comes easy. Ahmed and his friends didn't have time to spend their days worrying or trying to make sense of their lives. They had a mission. The mission gave their lives purpose. And that purpose was worth everything, in life and even more so in death.

Missiles and Mission

In April of 2017, I sat alone in my West Wing office waiting for the USS *Ross* and USS *Porter* to unleash a Tomahawk missile strike on a Syrian air base in retaliation for a chemical weapons attack perpetrated by the Assad regime. The strike would ultimately be successful, with fifty-eight out of fifty-nine missiles hitting their intended target; but as I waited, my mind drifted about 200 miles south of the targeted airbase to a village in northern Jordan.

That's where I was in the summer of 2015, sitting on the floor of a 550-square-foot apartment. The concrete walls were painted a dingy off-white. The floors were covered in thin, cracking gray tiles, and rust was beginning to corrode the apartment's heavy metal door around its edges. A thin silver tray holding miniature cups of coffee sat on the floor in the middle of the room. An early-2000s black TV sat in the corner on a wooden stand—the only piece of furniture in the entire apartment— airing Al Jazeera news reports on mute.

That tiny apartment was home to a family of seven. Two sisters—both in their thirties and wearing hijabs—lived together with five children between them: four boys, ages fourteen, twelve, seven, and two, and a three-year-old little girl. My wife, Megan, played with the younger kids, blowing bubbles and bouncing an inflatable ball as we talked. Until recently, they had been living in the Syrian city of Daraa, just north of the Jordanian border.

In 2010, as the so-called Arab Spring swept the Middle East, forcing Egyptian president Hosni Mubarak and Tunisian leader Zine El Abidine Ben Ali from office, many Syrians hoped their president—ophthalmologist turned dictator Bashar al-Assad—might be next. In early 2011, a group of boys in Daraa graffitied three words on the wall of their school: "your turn doctor." The "doctor," of course, was Assad. At the time, the teenage prank hardly seemed like the type of event that could spark a revolution, but Assad wasn't taking any chances. The regime arrested, imprisoned, and tortured twenty-three boys who were believed to have been involved in the graffiti incident. This prompted local protests, which led to a government crackdown and killings, which only spurred more protests. Eventually the government released the boys in an attempt to ease tensions. This worked, but only briefly. In the coming months, as the Syrian people revolted against their oppressors in greater and greater numbers, Daraa became a rebel stronghold, commonly known as "the cradle of the revolution."

One of the sisters, named Qamar, explained to me through a translator that even as the fighting grew more intense, they remained in their homes. "Our family had lived there for generations," she said. "It's our home. We didn't want to leave."

In April and May 2011, the Assad regime laid siege to Daraa. At one point, Qamar explained to me, tanks rolled through their neighborhood, and the battalion commander demanded that every fighting-age male renounce the revolution and join them, or face death. Her husband and other men in the neighborhood refused, prompting the Assad forces to bind them and lay them in the middle of the street in the path of the tanks. "We were pleading with the soldiers to let them live," she said, fighting back tears. "By the grace of God, the commander realized that my husband was his cousin, so he let him get up." The others were not so fortunate. The tanks slowly rolled over them all, one by one, leaving their lifeless bodies sunken into the gravel and mud below. The siege of Daraa ultimately left hundreds of protesters dead and as many as a thousand more in prison. Dozens of soldiers who defected, who could not bring themselves to carry out such atrocities, were slaughtered as well.

In the coming years, Daraa would remain a rebel stronghold during the ever-expanding Syrian civil war. ISIS overtook roughly half the country. Proxy battles broke out between Russian, Iranian, and American-backed forces, but the sisters and their families remained in Daraa. That is, until they just couldn't anymore.

"We stayed right up until the bombs reached our neighborhood," Qamar told me. The day they decided to leave, they rushed to pack whatever belongings they could carry. They hoped to catch a ride that evening on a flatbed truck bound for a refugee camp on the other side of the Jordanian border. They didn't make it in time, but this turned out to be a blessing in disguise.

"A bomb hit the truck," Qamar said, stone-faced. "Everyone was killed." Nearly the entire population of their neighborhood—all of their friends, and many of their family members—was lost in an instant.

They did catch a ride the following day, though, and made it to the Zaatari refugee camp. At the time, they were a group of ten. In addition to the seven I had met, the sisters were accompanied by their husbands and Qamar's elderly mother.

Living conditions were deplorable. They were piled on top of one another in white tents without air conditioning, at a time of year when daytime temperatures could hover as high as 113 degrees. Tragically, Qamar's mother succumbed to heatstroke just days after they had escaped the bombs.

Realizing they could no longer withstand the camp, they fled into Zarqa, a city of roughly a half million people, where displaced Syrian refugees were pouring into urban neighborhoods by the thousands. Qamar's husband, Ali, found work as a cook in a local restaurant, being paid under the table as an illegal. This type of arrangement bred intense resentment among the local population, whose jobs and wages were being undercut by the growing population of refugees desperate for work. I was immediately conscious of the parallels between this situation and the debate over illegal immigrant labor in the United States.

But Qamar was struggling to stretch her husband's income into even one meal a day for her family; they were withering away. Desperate and unable to find formula for their baby, Ali approached an imam at the neighborhood mosque and asked for help. That evening, Ali came home with a hopeful message for his wife: "The imam is going to help us find food." With their children sleeping on makeshift pallets across the room, empty stomachs growling with hunger, Qamar and Ali hugged each other a little closer that night, clinging to the hope that help was on the way. It wasn't. The following day, as Ali arrived for work at the restaurant, Jordanian security forces arrested him. As it turns out, the imam had not only decided he wouldn't help, he had turned Ali in to the police as an illegal worker, getting him deported back to Syria. The only reason his family had been able to stay was that Ali lied to the police, telling them he had no family in the country.

"What about your sister's husband?" I asked.

"He left the apartment one day and never came back," she said through the translator, rolling her eyes. "Jaban," she added with greater feeling. *Coward.*

At that point, my translator, Hasan, a Christian Jordanian national in his early thirties, interjected, first in Arabic and then in English. "And this is when we met," he said.

Qamar smiled and nodded, then explained that she had asked one of her neighbors—there were hundreds of Syrian refugees in their apartment complex—how they were making ends meet. They somehow always seemed to have food, and their kids even had a soccer ball to play with. With a mixture of bewilderment and awe, the neighbor explained that Hasan had been regularly bringing them enough food to get by. She offered to give Qamar his number, and later that afternoon, she skeptically reached out to him.

The following day, Hasan arrived on their doorstep with enough food and baby formula to last them for two weeks. And for the first time since she'd left her Syrian home behind, Qamar broke down in tears. She'd always wanted to stay strong for their children, she explained, so she refused to let herself cry—even as they lost their home and her mother, and were betrayed by their imam and separated from her husband. But the kindness of a total stranger, with whom she didn't share a nationality or religion, overwhelmed her emotions.

In the following months, she explained, Hasan and a small group of Jordanian Christians had taken care of them. They had spent countless hours talking about their families, their governments, and their dreams. Yes, even in the depths of despair, Qamar still had dreams. She dreamed of returning to her home. She dreamed of her children going back to school and playing soccer in the streets with their friends. She dreamed of going to sleep in a real bed, beside the husband she had not seen in over a year. They talked about their different faiths, and why a Christian was doing so much to help Muslims. And at some point, Qamar said, she had a revelation.

"My government failed me, my religion failed me," she said, "and when my family had no one else to turn to, the Christians were the only ones who didn't let us down." As a result of this entire experience, she asked Hasan how she could become a Christian. He told her, and now, months later, her entire family—including her husband back home in Syria—had converted.

Stories like this were the reason we traveled to the Middle East. We wanted to support the work that Hasan and his team were doing in Jordan. We wanted to help meet their physical needs, and hoped that by doing that, doors would be opened to meet their deeper, spiritual needs as well.

As James wrote in chapter 2 of his epistle:

What good is it, my brothers, if someone says he has faith but does not have works? Can that faith save him?

If a brother or sister is poorly clothed and lacking in daily food, and one of you says to them, "Go in peace, be warmed and filled," without giving them the things needed for the body, what good is that? So also faith by itself, if it does not have works, is dead.

We are saved by God's grace alone, through faith in Jesus alone. No amount of good works could ever earn our salvation. But as James continues in chapter 2, "I will show you my faith by my works." In other words, good works are evidence of the heart change that comes with true salvation.

I don't naturally have a servant's heart. I would much rather be served than serve. But something happens when I intentionally put myself in positions to serve other people; it bleeds over into every other aspect of my life. I'm suddenly more in tune with ways I can serve my wife or support my son. I become a better leader at the office because I'm not as fixated on my own ambitions. God has this whole thing rigged to create a virtuous cycle. The more time we spend on mission spreading the Gospel, the more we serve other people, the more we read the Bible and seek God's wisdom through prayer—the closer we'll be to him, the less we'll worry about the momentary challenges of life, and the more fulfilled we'll be.

Commander's Intent

Donald Trump is a memorable quote machine, but my favorite quote from my time in the White House was actually said by Secretary of Defense James Mattis. When CBS News anchor John Dickerson asked Mattis, a retired four-star Marine general, what kept him awake at night, he calmly replied, "Nothing. I keep other people awake at night." No wonder the president liked to call him "Mad Dog Mattis," a nickname Trump seemed to like more than Mattis did.

He was also known as the "warrior monk" because, throughout his military career, he would bring his roughly seven-thousand-volume library with him as he traveled from post to post. He said he did this so that even if an impending battle was the first time he'd encountered a certain set of variables and circumstances, he could rely on history to prepare him for it because, as Ecclesiastes 1:9 says, "There is nothing new under the sun."

Whenever there was an opportunity to pick his brain, I tried to take advantage of it. On one such occasion as we stood outside the Oval Office waiting for the president to finish a meeting and bring us in, Secretary Mattis launched into an explanation of "commander's intent." This is a well-known concept in the military that essentially boils down to everyone having a clear understanding of the team's goals and objectives. The U.S. Army field manual says commander's intent "succinctly describes what constitutes success for the operation. It includes the operation's purpose and the conditions that define the end state." If the commander has made it clear what success looks like, no one needs to be micromanaged along the way.

General Mattis recalled leading Marines into battle as they swept across Iraq on the way to Baghdad. To his memory, he gave only a handful of direct orders over the course of a few weeks. He'd made his intent clear, and his men were empowered to make the right decisions on how to achieve it as they went.

As soldiers in God's army—and in a battle to spread the Gospel in our culture—it's worth considering what our Commander's intent is.

Philippians 2:10–11 gives us a good starting point: "Every knee should bow, in heaven and on earth and under the earth, and every tongue confess that Jesus Christ is Lord, to the glory of God the Father."

And to achieve that end state, Jesus commanded us in Matthew 28:19–20:

> Go therefore and make disciples of all nations, baptizing them in the name of the Father and of the Son and of the Holy Spirit, teaching them to observe all that I have commanded you.

I've probably known these verses—commonly referred to as "The Great Commission"—since I was in elementary school. But not until my late twenties did I realize I had been subconsciously living as if those words don't actually apply to me.

Growing up, missionaries would come through our church about once a year and give a slide presentation showing their life and work in some exotic, remote, or seemingly dangerous place. The congregation would sit in rapt attention. Then the offering plate would get passed around, and we'd all drop a few extra dollars in the plate. And on the way out we'd shake their hands and think—and some might even say out loud—"Thank God they're called to do that! I'm not called to do that, but I'm glad someone is!"

This way of thinking is totally antithetical to our Commander's intent and his explicit orders.

Jesus commanded us, without any caveats, to "go" and "make disciples of all nations," every different people group, every clan, in every language. There's no ambiguity there. No one gets a free pass or a carve-out. It's not someone else's responsibility; it's each of ours. Anything short of total obedience to that call is sinful.

So how do we obey when, much like in General Mattis's explanation of commander's intent, the specifics are not spelled out in great detail, only the inevitable end state?

Jesus gave us a guide when he told his followers in his last words on Earth before ascending back to Heaven, "you will be my witnesses in Jerusalem and in all Judea and Samaria, and to the end of the earth" (Acts 1:8).

Using this model, it starts locally, sharing the Gospel in the everyday rhythms of life with our families, friends, co-workers, and other people we encounter. This means, too, that we pursue those in our life whom we view as "enemies," those we disagree with. Then the mission goes out from there. For some people, this means uprooting and relocating to another context, maybe even on the other side of the world. For others this means short-term trips to other contexts and prayers and financial support for longer-term work. In short, it can look a lot of different ways. But given the explicit nature of God's command to "go," should we not give deep consideration on an ongoing basis to what God's specific calling is for our lives—to what role he would have us play in executing his Great Commission?

What if we turned on its head the conventional approach of "I'll go if I'm called" and instead made it "I'll stay here if I'm called, otherwise I'm looking at opportunities to go to the nations"? That shift in mindset alone could change everything about how we spend our lives.

Shoot with Both Eyes Open

I was in a dead sprint like my life depended on it, but I felt like I was running in quicksand as a seventy-five-pound Belgian Malinois bore down on me from behind. The most terrifying sound I've ever heard was the dog's teeth clicking together moments before it latched on to my forearm and forced me to the ground as if it were trying to tear my shoulder out of socket.

The next sound I heard was hysterical laughter from a half dozen former members of Tier 1 Special Mission Units as the dog sank its teeth deep into my bite suit while I frantically—and hopelessly—tried to break free.

Over the course of several days in the backwoods of a southern U.S. state, I trained with these private military contractors for worst-case scenarios that might happen in some dark corner of the Earth.

I was ambushed during a hostage transfer and pelted with simulated bullets from lethal weapons systems that had been converted for training.

I got behind the wheel of a raggedy SUV and learned exactly how far I could push it without flipping it, feeling what it's like to ride on the thin line between control and disaster.

In the hand-to-hand combat and tactical knife fighting sessions, I was paired with a former Army soldier whose Special Operations unit is known as simply "The Activity" and whose operations were so sensitive you have to have code word clearance to even know where they'd been, much less what they were up to. My neck and rib cage still hurt thinking about it.

But the thing I remember most vividly is getting smacked across the head by a former Navy SEAL sniper. I had just let off the first couple of rounds from a .50-caliber rifle designed to hit targets over a mile away, and just as I was slowly squeezing the trigger to send another one down range, whack!

I jumped up instinctually with a look that must have screamed, "Dude! What's your problem?!," but not so aggressive to suggest that I was trying to escalate the situation with one of the toughest people on the planet.

"Shoot with both eyes open," he said calmly. "If you close one eye, you lose half your field of vision and you're setting yourself up to get blindsided."

Lesson learned, and not just when it comes to shooting. I've thought about that experience many times since then as a metaphor for what inevitably happens during my maniacal pursuit of whatever goal I'm obsessed with at the time. When I find something I want—typically something to do with attaining more money, power, or comfort—it's like I squint my eyes to focus on it alone. The first things to get eliminated from my field of vision are usually my daily time in the Word, my commitment to living in Biblical community with other believers, and any thought of spending my life on mission for the Gospel.

I've heard it said, "We plan, God laughs." But in my experience it's more like, "I plan without God and my plan gets my head knocked off." Not necessarily because my plans don't work, but because they often do "work" but don't bring any fulfillment, which can somehow be even more crushing than coming up short.

In James 4, the Bible warns, "Come now, you who say, 'Today or tomorrow we will go into such and such a town and spend a year there and trade and make a profit'—yet you do not know what tomorrow will bring. What is your life? For you are a mist that appears for a little time and then vanishes."

Planning our lives around, and devoting our lives to, earthly pursuits—success, power, politics—is a lot like shooting with one eye closed. Not only are we missing out entirely on God's infinite field of vision, we're allowing our own limited view of eternity to be obscured by the temporary "mist" of our earthly lives, which will soon vanish like a morning fog.

Notice, James didn't say, "Don't make any plans." He's saying that thinking our plans actually decide what's going to happen is just as foolish as not having a plan at all.

"Instead you ought to say, 'If the Lord wills, we will live and do this or that.'" James continues. "As it is, you boast in your arrogance. All such boasting is evil."

From Crack House to the White House

One Sunday afternoon while sitting at my desk in the West Wing, a friend texted me a picture of an article from *Street Sense*, a newspaper focused on Washington, D.C.'s homeless community. Many of the writers are homeless or formerly homeless. The article that had been sent to me was by a gentleman named Jeffery McNeil, a once-homeless Trump supporter who had turned his life around.

On a whim, I decided to invite him to the White House to hear more about his backstory. Several days later in the West Wing lobby I met Mr. McNeil, a middle-aged black man who insisted I call him "Jeff," and he shared with me his unforgettable story.

Roughly a decade before our unlikely meeting, Jeff had arrived in Washington, D.C., with nothing more than the clothes on his back and thirty dollars in his pocket. He was addicted to drugs and alcohol and had lost most of his money buying illicit substances and gambling. Like many in D.C.'s large homeless community, he spent most nights sleeping near Franklin Square, a large green space several blocks from the White House with the massive *Washington Post* building towering over its north side.

To escape from the elements during the day, Jeff frequented nearby public libraries. He was barely literate, but if he read quietly and kept to himself, he was generally allowed to stay as long as he wanted. Over time, he became a prolific reader. He moved on from more elementary texts to books about politics, economics, and philosophy. The more Jeff learned, the more he wanted to share his newfound knowledge with others, and so he began submitting articles to *Street Sense* in the hope of getting published. "I'll never forget the first time I finally saw something I'd written in print," he recalled with pride. Jeff's passion turned into a business opportunity as well. He started selling newspapers during the day, increasing his circulation and putting hard-earned money in his pocket.

As we walked out of the West Wing and down the West Colonnade by the Rose Garden, Jeff told me that selling newspapers had allowed him to save up enough money to get off the street. He'd rented a small apartment nearby and was working a second job, in addition to writing and selling papers. Stopping to soak in the view, Jeff became reflective.

"Everyone's worth something, you know?" he said. "Too many people have forgotten that their life is worth something—they matter, they can have a purpose."

Several days later I grabbed a *Street Sense* newspaper from a vendor near the White House and opened it up to the opinion section, hoping that Jeff had written about his experience.

"From the crack house to the White House," the headline blared.[1] I smiled.

Jeff was right. Everyone's life is worth something. In fact, it's worth so much "that while we were still sinners, Christ died for us" (Romans 5:6–8). How much different would our interactions be if we went through our days cognizant of the fact that every person we speak to is worth so much to God that he sacrificed his Son to save them? How would we interact with those with whom we disagree—on politics, theology, or whatever? I know my interactions would be dramatically different.

The barrier to that mindset is that we have a warped view of worth. The world says you're worth something because of how awesome you are. The Bible says you're worth something because of how awesome Christ is.

At a fundamental level, sin is wanting something more than we want Jesus. If we can't bring ourselves to put Jesus' supreme worth in its proper place in our life's hierarchy (that is, he is everything, he is enough) and then derive our self-worth from the glory of the cross, then how will we ever be able to view others as God sees them?

"Christ Jesus came into the world to save sinners" (1 Timothy 1:15). And since "all have sinned" (Romans 3:23), that means Christ Jesus came into the world to save you, me, and every person with whom we come in contact. Once that worldview penetrates our hearts, the only natural response is to share that good news with every person we can so that they too can receive the gift of finding their true worth in Christ—the only sense of worth that will ever be truly fulfilling and never fade.

The Power of Life and Death

"Do you ever tweet out and wake up and be like, 'Oh man, I wish I didn't send that one out'?"

Sitting on the Rose Garden Patio just outside the Oval Office, Dave Portnoy asked what a lot of interviewers had probably thought to themselves but never quite articulated to President Trump in those terms.

"Often. Too often," the president replied. "It used to be, in the old days, you'd write a letter, and you'd say, 'This letter's really big.' You'd put it on your desk, and then you go back tomorrow and you say, 'Oh, I'm glad I didn't send it,' right? But we don't do that with Twitter, right? We put it out instantaneously, we feel great, and then you start getting phone calls: 'Did you really say this?'"

As I watched the interview unfold, I laughed to myself thinking about all the times a presidential tweet or off-the-cuff comment had sent my day in an unexpected direction. While I was working in the White House, the second I woke up in the morning my heart would race as I frantically grabbed my phone to see what the president had said either late the night before or very early that morning. But I also thought about all the times my own mouth had gotten me in trouble over the years—both inside and outside the White House.

A University of Arizona study found that the average person speaks about 16,000 words per day.[2] That's roughly the length of this book every three days. I'd be interested to know what percentage of those words are thoughtful, meaningful, encouraging, and loving. If an audio recorder captured my unguarded comments all day and replayed them aloud, I shudder to think what people would say.

Words are easy to just throw out there. So easy, in fact, that we can easily forget how powerful they are. As the author writes in Proverbs 18, "Death and life are in the power of the tongue." Words have launched wars, genocides, and other atrocities. They have also destroyed marriages, ended friendships, estranged families, and derailed careers.

The word "fool" appears three times in Proverbs 18, each time describing someone who's talking more than they're listening. "A fool takes no pleasure in understanding, but only in expressing his opinion... A fool's lips walk into a fight, and his mouth invites a beating. A fool's mouth is his ruin, and his lips are a snare to his soul." There are a lot of fools yapping on cable "news" programs. I know this for certain because sometimes I've been one of them.

The good news is that the power of words cuts the other way as well. "A gentle tongue is a tree of life" (Proverbs 15:4). "The tongue of the wise brings healing" (Proverbs 12:18). Words can inspire hope, build up the downtrodden, and make peace. They can ask for—and grant—forgiveness.

We could all benefit from being more thoughtful and gracious with our words. But this doesn't mean we're soft or shy away from speaking God's truth into a culture that will respond with hostility.

Jesus was meek (the original Greek word is *praus*, loosely meaning strength under control), not weak. The Jesus who was moved to tears to find his followers mourning the death of a friend (John 11) is the same Jesus who described the scribes and Pharisees as "hypocrites" and a "brood of vipers" (Matthew 23), "overturned the tables of the money changers" in the temple (Matthew 21), and willingly laid down his life in the most excruciating way imaginable. So while we need to deliver our words with grace, humility, and intentionality, we also need to pray for the boldness to speak up in situations when it would be much easier—and cost us a lot less—to keep quiet.

Ultimately our words are a window into our souls, "for out of the abundance of the heart [the] mouth speaks" (Luke 6:45). What do your words say about the condition of your heart?

Tax Cuts for Christmas

It was a cold, crisp December afternoon, and I was waiting for President Trump in the State Dining Room with my White House colleague Tony Sayegh. The president was on his way over to deliver a speech advocating for the largest tax cut in a generation, and it was coming down to the wire. He'd promised to deliver "tax cuts for Christmas," but negotiations were tense, and we weren't sure we'd be able to round up the votes in Congress. Tony and I—and numerous others on the White House staff—had devoted the last five months of our lives to this effort.

Just then, my phone vibrated in my pocket, breaking the nervous tension. One of our lead negotiators on Capitol Hill was calling with big news: they'd finally had a breakthrough.

"You should consider updating the remarks, because we've

got a deal," he told me. "The bill is going to pass. The president should announce it first, before anyone on the Hill can."

I hung up and looked over at Tony, who was pacing nervously while reading a copy of the president's prepared remarks. Through an open door I heard three buzzes, signaling that the president was getting on his private elevator to come up to where we were waiting. My heart rate picked up slightly.

In the thirty seconds between that moment and the president's walking in the room, we identified the key line in the speech that needed tweaking: "As we speak, Congress is putting the finishing touches on a plan" needed to be changed to "Congress has reached an agreement on tax legislation..."

The president glided into the room as Tony marked through the old line and scribbled in the updated language.

"What've we got, guys?" he said, looking back and forth between Tony and me.

"Mr. President, this is going to be the speech everyone remembers about the tax bill," I began. "You're going to be the first to announce that Congress has reached an agreement on the final bill. It's going to pass."

Tony handed him his copy of the remarks with the updated language, and Trump squinted to read Tony's chicken-scratch handwriting.

"You okay with this?" I asked.

He nodded his approval, and I ran off to have the sentence updated in the teleprompter.

Minutes later, Trump stepped up to the podium centered

between four towering white marble columns in the White House's grand Entrance Hall. To his left and right were a dozen perfectly triangular Christmas trees, covered in silver tinsel and faux white snow. Directly behind him, the door leading into the Blue Room was left open so the official White House Christmas tree could be seen inside.

As he began speaking, I ducked into the White House usher's office to see what the scene looked like on TV. People all over the country must have thought the president was delivering his remarks from some kind of winter wonderland. Tax cuts for Christmas. It was perfect.

I walked back out to the Cross Hall to watch from the president's left, just out of sight of the cameras, with the famous painting of JFK deep in thought just over my right shoulder. It was the most exciting moment of my entire time in the White House. Nearly every person in the country would be impacted by this effort we'd been a part of, and it's still considered President Trump's signature legislative achievement. But for me, it was accompanied by an unexpected—and at the time, unexplainable—air of melancholy.

I slowly surveyed the scene I was standing in—one that very few kids from Alabama will ever get to witness—and thought to myself that I might never again in my career be part of something of this magnitude. It's a strange thing to ponder the possibility that you've reached your professional peak in your early thirties.

But the truth is, many of life's biggest moments leave us feeling small, insignificant, and unfulfilled. And that's by God's design. Even the short-term sugar-rush of happiness we might get from "winning" or "achieving" is fleeting, because we weren't made for those moments—the ones where we "did" something, where we're a big deal, even if only in our own minds. As theologian John Piper said, "deeply written on the human soul is the truth that we were made, not to be made much of, but to make much of God."

Moments that make me bigger will never satisfy my hunger for meaning, because God hard-wired each of us so that we are only "complete in Him" (Colossians 2:10).

"He must increase, but I must decrease," John the Baptist famously said (John 3:30).

I thought I felt this subtle sadness because I might have "peaked." But upon further reflection, I wasn't fearful that my career had reached its pinnacle, but that no career peak, no matter how high, would ever be enough. For the first time I acutely felt Jesus' words in Matthew 16, "what will it profit a man if he gains the whole world and forfeits his soul?"

If the most remarkable thing anyone can say about me is that I reached the pinnacle of a profession—any profession—I will have wasted my life. This revelation flies in the face of every "self-help" podcast I've listened to and nearly every personal development book I've read.

While languishing in prison, Paul wrote, "to live is Christ, and to die is gain" (Philippians 1:21). So if Christ is glorified in what I do, then I will have achieved my true purpose. And when I die, I will be with God in heaven, the ultimate gain!

In the meantime, "I count everything as loss because of the surpassing worth of knowing Christ Jesus my Lord" (Philippians 3:8).

Back in the White House, the moment was over as quickly
as it began. As President Trump stepped back onto the elevator,
he flashed a thumbs-up at me as the doors slid shut.

Heirs to the King

The only thing more hardcore than partisan politics is SEC
sports. For years now I've had a running back-and-forth with
Sarah Huckabee Sanders: If the University of Alabama beats the
University of Arkansas in anything—from football to thumb
wrestling, and anything in between—she can count on me
sending her a message about it, and vice versa. So when I joked
to Sarah that I had begrudgingly decided to endorse her candi-
dacy for governor of Arkansas, she sent me a message back that
the only Alabama endorsement she would accept was from my
son, Shep. "Because even though he's brainwashed in all things
'Roll Tide,' he's too cute not to love, so that's the condition!"

I'm sure she didn't think about it, but her mentioning Shep
was sort of a full-circle moment. Five years earlier I had stood
in her West Wing office and gotten emotional talking about my
wife, Megan, going through fertility treatments, a years-long
journey that ultimately led to us adopting Shep.

For most of my life, anytime I thought about adoption—
which was almost never—it struck me as a superhuman act of
self-sacrifice, something hard to imagine even attempting to

take on. Too difficult to take on. It's one of many ignorant views on adoption I innocently held for the first thirty-plus years of my life. Another psychological barrier I had was the thought that would-be adoptive parents struggle with wondering—and rarely saying aloud—whether they would fully love an adopted child the way they would a biological child.

While I was still working in the White House, Megan went on a short-term mission trip to Africa and spent a lot of time in an orphanage there. God used that experience to help her overcome her fears and spur her heart toward starting an adoption process of our own. But it wasn't without some challenges along the way.

Medical records for orphans in many countries can be hit-or-miss. Our son was diagnosed with two significant health issues shortly after he was born, but there was conflicting information from different times and different doctors. After looking through all the medical records and scans, an American doctor who specializes in adoptions told us, "He may have no serious medical issues whatsoever, or he may need you to take care of him every day for the rest of his life."

It wasn't a hard decision to go forward with the process because we knew in our hearts that he was already our son. And he can know forever that we always wanted him, no matter what. This, as it turns out, is particularly important. For years after he joined our family, he would randomly ask in his tiny voice, "You'll never leave me?" or "You always come back?" And when he's old enough to fully understand, he'll know that we really meant the answers to those questions before we even met him for the first time.

Like many parents, having a child radically changed my perspective on my relationship with God. It's a daunting task to fully embrace and attempt to implement Paul's exhortation to "follow me as I follow Christ" (1 Corinthians 11:1 MEV). In moments when my son's disobedience tests the limits of my patience, I often can't help but think about the endless grace God has extended to me without exasperation. But more than anything, Shep's adoption story has opened my eyes to the doctrine of adoption that is at the heart of the Gospel. All believers have been adopted by the living God, with all the rights that come with being a child of the King.

"For all who are led by the Spirit of God are sons of God. For you did not receive the spirit of slavery to fall back into fear, but you have received the Spirit of adoption as sons, by whom we cry, 'Abba! Father!' The Spirit himself bears witness with our spirit that we are children of God, and if children, then heirs—heirs of God and fellow heirs with Christ, provided we suffer with him in order that we may also be glorified with him" (Romans 8:14–17).

Few things on Earth are a clearer illustration of the Gospel than adoption. Our God is "Father to the fatherless" (Psalm 68:5). In promising to send his Spirit to be with his followers after completing his earthly ministry, Jesus said, "I will not leave you as orphans; I will come to you" (John 14:18).

Adopting our son has been the single most rewarding

experience I've ever had. If you haven't ever considered adoption, you're not only missing out on the incredible joy and blessing an adopted child will be in your home; you're also missing out on an opportunity to display the Gospel message in a unique way for everyone in your life. That's at least worth praying about.

The Only Throne Room That Matters

In the "Great Man" theory of history, the course of human events is said to be largely determined by the impact of highly influential individuals who, by sheer force of will, personality, or talent, reshape the world in their image. While working in the White House, I interacted with numerous government and business leaders whom some historians might consider to be such men. Some of them clearly considered themselves to be such men, too.

President Trump is the obvious example, but there were others. Israeli Prime Minister Benjamin Netanyahu positioned himself as a modern-day Winston Churchill, a defender of the West with a belligerent Iran playing the role of Hitler's Germany. I watched Elon Musk, who spends his time revolutionizing the automotive industry and trying to make the human species multi-planetary, pitch the president on an underground high-speed train idea. I bumped into Amazon founder Jeff Bezos outside the Situation Room. And I recall the Saudi delegation as Crown Prince Mohammed bin Salman met with the president to discuss everything from a giant military arms deal to his plans to modernize his father's kingdom. This is one of the extraordinary things about working in the West Wing: if someone is there to meet the president, they're typically at the top of their field.

These "great" men—and others I met, including some powerful women—all had to make enormous decisions every day. Some of their decisions were matters of life and death, and others shaped the global order or dictated the flow of billions, even trillions of dollars. Despite all of their power, influence, and even success, you and I are on equal footing with these so-called greats. In fact, some of them have clearly and openly made the wrong decision when it comes to the most important decision of all: whom they will serve. So while they may be remembered for generations, or even celebrated, for their worldly exploits, they may find themselves on the wrong side of the only matter that will stand the ultimate test—the test of eternity.

So much of our day-to-day lives—even the "good" things—are conducted without an eternal perspective. We strive, we struggle, we grasp, we achieve. We make an impact on our businesses, our friends, our families, and our communities. We create a legacy that others aspire to emulate. We build our kingdoms. But what about *the* Kingdom? Paul gives a great perspective on this in Philippians 3: "[W]hatever gain I had, I counted as loss for the sake of Christ. Indeed, I count everything as loss because of the surpassing worth of knowing Christ Jesus my Lord. For his sake I have suffered the loss of all things and count them as rubbish, in order that I may gain Christ."

So in the end, when all of the superfluous, earthly things are stripped away, what will a life spent for the sake of Christ look like? Theologian and author D. A. Carson sums it up perfectly in his biography of his father, Tom Carson, whom he called "a most ordinary pastor."

"When he died, there were no crowds outside the hospital, no editorial comments in the papers, no announcements on television, no mention in Parliament, no attention paid by the nation. In his hospital room there was no one by his bedside. There was only the quiet hiss of oxygen, vainly venting because he had stopped breathing and would never need it again. But on the other side all the trumpets sounded. Dad won entrance to the only throne room that matters, not because he was a good man or a great man . . . but because he was a forgiven man."[3]

CHAPTER 4

The Valley: Suffering, Weakness, Persecution, and Grace

The afternoon of March 1, 2007, I was at a local restaurant in Enterprise, Alabama, a prototypical small southern town, where I was living at the time. It was an overcast day, and thunderstorms—and perhaps even tornadoes—were on the way. If you've never lived in an area where tornadoes are a regular part of life, it may seem strange that tornado watches don't necessarily spark anxiety among the locals. Familiarity erodes urgency.

In pretty much every place I lived growing up, the first day of each month included a mandatory test of the local tornado siren, which would wail for a few minutes in loud and soft waves as its horn rotated slowly atop a tower. Even when there actually were legitimate tornado warnings, if the siren went off at night,

I'd get annoyed that it woke me up, then just roll over and go back to sleep. If it went off during the day, I'd turn up the TV so I could hear whatever show I was watching over the horn.

But on this Thursday afternoon, that was about to change.

At 12:45 p.m. that day, a tornado warning was issued for Coffee County, including the City of Enterprise. Eighteen minutes later, a massive EF-4 tornado touched down in Enterprise. Five minutes later, after briefly lifting off the ground, it touched back down and obliterated the town's high school, where students were huddled in hallways, crouched with their heads tucked down. As the tornado hit, there was sudden darkness in the school's brightly lit hallways. Then chaos and screaming. Then silence.

From where I was watching, we could see the tornado throwing a mountain of debris into the sky as it devastated everything in its path. Once it lifted back off the ground and dissipated back into the ether, I walked outside into the eerie calm of an orange-tinted haze.

Then suddenly, the concussion of a shock wave took my breath away. About 200 yards in front of me, an electrical substation had exploded, sending a tower of fire into the sky—like the Eye of Sauron—so hot that I could feel it on my skin as I squinted my eyes from the distance of two football fields.

Knowing my dad's office at Hillcrest Baptist Church was near the path of the tornado, right across the street from the high school, I jumped in my car and sped that way. The streets were littered with downed power lines, and familiar houses were...just...gone. Wiped clean from the face of the Earth.

When I made it to the church, it was like a scene out of *War of the Worlds*. The church was untouched, but across the street, hundreds of students—some running, others walking, others stumbling—were streaming out of the mayhem, like a giant blender had stretched down from the sky and turned steel, concrete, and brick into a horrific cake batter.

My dad, a former firefighter, was running between the school and our church helping kids find their way. Emergency triage was being set up inside the church's fellowship hall. Cell phone service was choked off as everyone in town simultaneously tried to find out if their loved ones were okay.

In the coming hours, parents would flood to the scene searching for their kids. As daylight turned to dusk, some stared aimlessly at the wreckage. The steady stream of students slowed to a trickle, then stopped, and even as they held out hope, they knew they had likely hugged their babies for the last time.

Eight students died that day when, as they crouched in the hallway, a concrete wall collapsed and crushed them. One of the boys fought to hold up a concrete beam so another student could escape. He gave his life for his friend.

When it was all over, the tornado had cut a path through town 200 yards wide and ten miles long. Nine people were dead—the eight students and an elderly woman who died at her home nearby.

Two days later, I met a president of the United States for the first time.

When George W. Bush heard about the tragedy and saw the devastation, he came to offer his condolences and support in person. "We can never replace lives, and we can't heal hearts, except through prayer," he said. "I want the students to know, and the families to know that there's a lot of people praying for them." When he arrived at our church, he met one-on-one with the families who had lost children. No cameras. No fanfare. No crocodile tears—they were the real deal.

He also met a high school senior that day named Megan Parks, the student body president, who helped show him around the school and stood with him as he talked to the media about what he'd seen. Today, seventeen years later, Megan is my wife and still cannot recall many of the details from that time period. Trauma does such strange things to the body, mind, and memory.

And so does grief. No parent or high school student who lost a child or friend that day was ever quite the same. But the paths their lives took after that tragic, formative moment diverged widely. Some were consumed by the loss and never fully re-emerged on the other side. Others overcame the unimaginable sadness and drew closer to the people they loved—and to God.

But many—all across the spectrum of brokenness and resilience—were left to wrestle with a singular question: Why?

In the depths of our suffering, when our weakness is laid bare before the world or when our world has been broken—whether from the loss of a loved one, a global pandemic, or even the breaking up of a church or community—is God's grace really enough?

The Nine-Year-Old's Prayer Chain

About a year into my time in the White House, press secretary Sarah Huckabee Sanders texted me an article about a nine-year-old girl from Texas named Sophia. This beautiful little brown-haired girl was suffering from a rare disease that kept her brain from getting enough blood. She had endured numerous strokes and multiple surgeries. In preparation for her next operation, Sophia told her mom she wanted "the whole world" to pray for her, which in her young mind meant "10,000 people." Sarah wanted to make sure we helped Sophia exceed that goal.

It didn't take long for me to track down a phone number for Sophia's mom, Karyn. So I called and asked if we could share Sophia's story during the White House press briefing, and urge people watching to pray for her.

"Sophia, it's the White House on the phone," Karyn told her daughter. "They want to know if you'd be okay with the whole country joining your prayer chain." Sophia agreed that this sounded like a good idea, so the next week—three days before her surgery—Sarah shared Sophia's story during the nationally televised White House press briefing.

"Sophia, I'm here to tell you that millions of people from every corner of the world will be praying for you," Sarah said, trying to keep her emotions at bay. "And among those people will be all of us here at the White House."

A few days later, after a successful operation, President Trump decided he wanted Sophia to be his special guest at the upcoming National Prayer Breakfast. And less than two weeks after her life was hanging in the balance, I watched Sophia, who doctors at one point said would never walk again, run into the arms of the president of the United States for a hug.

A few years later, I looked Sophia up to see what she was up to. I found her on social media,[1] and in her first few posts was an image of Romans 8:31. "If God is for us, who can be against us?"

This immediately grabbed my attention. How could a preteen post such a thing, even as a terrible disease had been ravaging her body for years? Perhaps it's because she had a deeper understanding of what it actually means for God to be "for us" than most people do—and it doesn't mean that everything will always go our way or that we'll never experience pain.

We are sinners living in a fallen world. Suffering is inevitable. It will come for us all. Cancer may come for our bodies. Alzheimer's may come for our minds. Tragedy may come for our loved ones. Betrayal may come for our friendships. And natural disasters may come for our homes. Is God no longer for us in these moments?

The key to answering this question can actually be found just a few verses before the one Sophia posted, in Romans 8:28: "And we know that for those who love God all things work together for good…"

"All things" includes even—and perhaps especially—our suffering. We may not understand it at the moment. But the second we start questioning God's greatness or goodness, Romans 8:28 is an ever-present reminder that he is sovereign; he can be trusted. He is working in the midst of our suffering for our good and for his glory.

Nowhere is this more evident than in the picture of Jesus crucified on the cross. To orchestrate the redemption of all mankind, God ordained the murder of his own son. Jesus took the weight of all sin and sacrificed himself as the ultimate picture of God's grace and love for everyone. Or as Isaiah put it, "By his stripes, we are healed" (Isaiah 53:5 MEV).

Now our perspective can change. Our earthly pain is an indispensable opportunity to share in Christ's suffering. It can be used for God's glory by building up our faith and sanctifying us. This is how Paul—who was imprisoned numerous times, beaten, stoned, shipwrecked, left hungry and thirsty, cold and exposed—could write that "the sufferings of this present time are not worth comparing with the glory that is to be revealed to us" (Romans 8:18).

Our suffering is not meaningless. God promises to give us all the grace and strength we need to endure our momentary pain, knowing that the splendor of eternity is waiting. Who, therefore, can be against us? No one. Because even in death, we are transported into the presence of the Father.

So as Job put it, "Though he slay me, I will hope in him" (Job 13:15).

The Lie Detector

Taking a polygraph—or, as some call it, a "lie detector" test—ranks among the most miserable experiences of my life. Even as you're reading this, I bet memories are flooding into your mind about things you've done that you'd prefer to never have to discuss with anyone. Unfortunately for me, passing a polygraph exam is a requirement to attain the U.S. government's highest security clearance, which is a prerequisite to working in the Office of the Director of National Intelligence.

I can't get into many of the details of the tradecraft behind the polygraph examination. They make it clear that taking a polygraph is kind of like *Fight Club*; the first rule is that you don't talk about it once you leave. But I'll just say that those embarrassing things you're thinking about right now would probably come up.

Can they actually tell if you're being truthful? Who knows. The machine measures various physiological reactions your body makes as you answer questions, like your heart rate, or the way you shift in the chair, or your breathing and perspiration. Then the examiner is trained to read between the lines of all those data points and assess your credibility. The science behind these tests isn't perfect; they're typically not even admissible as evidence in court. But if you want a job handling the government's most sensitive secrets, your best bet is to just tell the truth.

Polygraph literally means "many writings" or "many pictures." I guess it's like a word cloud or collage of your mind, which is a fascinating if not terrifying thing to consider. But if that's scary, then 1 John 3:20 is downright horrifying: "[God] knows everything." He is "perfect in knowledge" (Job 37:16) and is always "discerning the thoughts and intentions of the heart" (Hebrews 4:12). He's "testing" our purity the way that a crucible and furnace separate silver and gold from rubbish (Proverbs 17:3).

Yikes! As I consider these verses, two things come to mind.

First, in our day-to-day lives, we don't feel the weight of sin as much as we should. I was so exhausted after my polygraph exam that I drove straight home and just went to sleep. Getting tested and being vulnerable like that is uncomfortable. But God is doing that nonstop with 100 percent accuracy. He not only sees the secret, embarrassing things we've done, he knows the darkest desires of our hearts. And yet we go on sinning against the God of the universe, knowing full well he's watching it happen in the moment.

Second, I think of the popular Christian song that declares to God with an appropriate sense of wonder, "I'm fully known and loved by You." In spite of knowing all of our nastiest parts, Romans 8:1–2 reminds us that there is "no condemnation for those who are in Christ Jesus. For the law of the Spirit of life has set you free in Christ Jesus from the law of sin and death."

So while we should constantly remind ourselves of the seriousness of sin, we should also remember that the shame that often accompanies it—even after seeking forgiveness—is a feeling that comes from Satan, not God. What extraordinary hope there is in the promise that "as far as the east is from the west, so far does he remove our transgressions from us" (Psalm 103:12).

Ask God to search your heart and expose the sinful parts you haven't yet turned over to him, and thank him for his unfailing love—shown in all its glory in the form of Jesus on the cross—that ensures you will one day stand before him and be found righteous.

The White House and Weakness

I sat quietly in the southwest corner of the Cabinet Room in the West Wing of the White House. Charles Willson Peale's 1776 portrait of General George Washington, commissioned by John Hancock, hung just above my head. Senior national security officials were assembled around the long wooden table for a bilateral meeting between President Trump and Egypt's President Abdel Fattah el-Sisi.

One of the things President Trump loved to do in these meetings was introduce his team, which included the most famous military general of his generation and numerous billionaire titans of industry. Among the group of business icons flanking Trump was Gary Cohn, the former president of Goldman Sachs, Wall Street's most famous investment bank. Cohn was now Trump's top economic advisor.

The president pointed at Gary and leaned forward toward the Egyptian delegation with a mischievous grin on his face. "He made a few hundred million dollars and had to pay a lot

My childhood home in south Jackson, Mississippi. *(Photo courtesy of Cliff Sims)*

My first book tour included stops in some hostile environments, but Stephen Colbert told me right before I walked out onstage for *The Late Show* that if his audience heckled or booed me, he would stop the segment and tell them "That's not how we treat our guests." *(Photo courtesy of Cliff Sims)*

Every seat in the staff cabin of Air Force One has a phone. My first call was to my grandfather. *(Photo by Dan Scavino)*

Off-camera in the Oval Office while the president was conducting a video call with astronauts aboard the International Space Station, I was watching the clock and preparing to signal to the president that it was time to wrap it up. *(Photo courtesy of Cliff Sims)*

Walking into the office with the president in the morning, probably talking about the stories driving the news that day. *(Official White House Photo by Shelah Craighead)*

Sharing a laugh with the president in the Cabinet Room. *(Official White House Photo by Shelah Craighead)*

Walking down the West Colonnade between the White House residence and the West Wing late in the Trump Administration when I had come back as Deputy Director of National Intelligence for Strategy and Communications. *(Official White House Photo by Shelah Craighead)*

Moments before the president was set to deliver nationally televised remarks, I got a call that we'd reached a deal to pass the Trump tax cuts through Congress. We scrambled to update his remarks so he could be the first to announce the deal. *(Official White House Photo by Shelah Craighead)*

My official photo from the Office of the Director of National Intelligence. *(Official U.S. Government photo)*

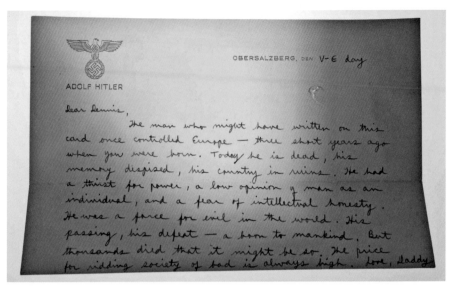

OBERSALZBERG, DEN V-E day

ADOLF HITLER

Dear Dennis,

The man who might have written on this card once controlled Europe — three short years ago when you were born. Today he is dead, his memory despised, his country in ruins. He had a thirst for power, a low opinion of man as an individual, and a fear of intellectual honesty. He was a force for evil in the world. His passing, his defeat — a boon to mankind. But thousands died that it might be so. The price for ridding society of bad is always high. Love, Daddy.

I would periodically visit a museum tucked into a corner of the CIA's headquarters to view this letter. In the waning days of WWII, future CIA Director Richard Helms, then an intelligence officer, was among the first Americans to get inside Adolf Hitler's mountaintop retreat. He obtained Hitler's personal stationery and on it wrote this letter to his son, Dennis. Over a half-century later, the day after Osama bin Laden was killed in a CIA-led operation in Pakistan, Dennis Helms donated his dad's letter to the CIA Museum as an ever-present reminder that "the price of ridding society of bad is always high." *(Official CIA Photo)*

Recording the president's weekly address in the Diplomatic Reception Room of the White House. The practice, started by Franklin D. Roosevelt and later revived by Ronald Reagan, didn't get much attention in recent years until Trump's unpredictable approach sometimes garnered millions of views online, or as he would put it, "great ratings!" *(Official White House Photo by Shelah Craighead)*

Visiting the U.S.-Mexico border, Yuma Sector, where Mexican cartels smuggle drugs and people into the United States at a scale that is hard to fathom until seeing it firsthand. *(Photo courtesy of Cliff Sims)*

In what now seems like an entire lifetime ago in the mid-2000s, I was a professional musician, touring around the country playing in a large venue or arena one week and small clubs the next. Sometimes we'd share the stage with chart-topping bands and gather around televisions to hear our songs on MTV; other times we'd be on tour in a van for months playing with indie bands in front of tiny crowds. *(Photo by Max Oden)*

Walking (left, in red) through a city in the Middle East, where we visited local Christians who daily put themselves at risk to share the gospel with Muslim refugees who fled the chaos, death, and destruction of the Syrian civil war. *(Photo courtesy of Cliff Sims)*

of taxes to come work here, but he did it," he said. "Thanks, Gary, the U.S. Treasury appreciates it." Cohn just laughed and nodded.

Most people around the table probably didn't know that Gary was far from the most likely person to rise to such lofty heights, especially since his job was dealing with numbers. He had struggled his way through school with dyslexia, at a time when educators were still figuring out how to best serve such students. In a bestselling book that shared Gary's remarkable story, he revealed that even to this day he reads at a pace of fewer than four pages per hour.[2] But he had a well-earned reputation for being "one tough cookie," as the president put it. And while he was in the White House, he helped orchestrate the largest tax cuts and reforms in almost forty years.

Our limitations and weaknesses can feel debilitating, and particularly in a world driven by power and success. But paradoxically, the root of that feeling of insecurity or insufficiency is actually pride, because it assumes that our opportunity to contribute to the Kingdom is dependent on our human ability, not God's grace.

Just look at Biblical history.

Moses is known as the bold leader who stood up to Pharaoh, led the Israelites out of slavery, parted the Red Sea, and received the Ten Commandments directly from God atop Mount Sinai. But before that he was so crippled with insecurity over his inability to speak eloquently—and perhaps even a speech impediment—that he complained to God that he was "slow of speech and of tongue." God reassured him, "I will be with your mouth and teach you what you shall speak" (Exodus 4).

David was a small boy who didn't look anything like a mighty warrior or leader of men. During Samuel's search for a new king, God had to tell him to ignore the physical stature of one of David's brothers who looked more the part (1 Samuel 16:7). Yet David would go on to slay Goliath (1 Samuel 17) because he knew where his power came from: "The Lord is my strength and my shield" (Psalm 28:6).

The apostle Paul wrote large portions of the New Testament. But he also "pleaded with the Lord" to remove an unnamed weakness, which he referred to as "a thorn" so bad he called it "a messenger of Satan to harass me." God's response to Paul was "My grace is sufficient for you, for my power is made perfect in weakness" (2 Corinthians 12).

Our weaknesses make us more humble and remind us that we are entirely dependent upon God. They also encourage us to live in community by increasing our need and appreciation for others. And they give us a natural way to empathize with and minister to others when they are struggling.

So rather than feeling inadequate or hiding your weaknesses today, consider taking Paul's approach:

Therefore I will boast all the more gladly of my weaknesses, so that the power of Christ may rest upon me. For the sake of Christ, then, I am content with weaknesses, insults, hardships, persecutions, and calamities.

For when I am weak, then I am strong (2 Corinthians 12: 9–10).

Criticism and the Smartest Person I've Ever Met

Elon Musk is without question the smartest person I met while working in the White House, a time in which I met kings, conversed with princes, dined with diplomats, and shook hands with some of the wealthiest people in human history. In almost every one of those experiences, even when I walked away impressed, I harbored the same nagging feeling: they're not any smarter than me—or you, or most people that we hang out with or work alongside.

Elon was the exception; he was clearly operating on a different intellectual plane than the rest of us mere mortals.

One afternoon in the White House, Elon was among a group of business leaders Trump had invited in to discuss the country's crumbling infrastructure. Trump went around the Cabinet Room soliciting ideas and feedback from his guests, finally making his way to Musk. "Elon, what do you have for us?" he asked, giving Musk the floor.

"Mr. President, I'd like to discuss a way to take people from Washington, D.C., to New York City in twenty-nine minutes by tunneling," he began. "There's no reason we should be okay with sitting in traffic all day...We can fix this." He went on to explain that he was developing technology to transport people at up to seven hundred miles per hour in underground tubes known as hyperloops. "It's a high-density area, so we'll want to remain underground the entire way," he said. "It will take right at twenty-nine minutes."

All eyes in the room swung back to the president to see how he would react to a proposal that was so wildly different from any other ideas that had been thrown out so far. "Everyone else is talking about bridges and roads, and this guy comes in here talking about tunnels and this and that!" the president exclaimed, sitting back in his chair and drawing laughter from the group. "That's good, Elon," he concluded. "Do it. I wish you the best of luck." There wasn't any further discussion on the topic, and several of the executives in the room seemed to be exchanging skeptical glances.

But one of the things I respect about Elon Musk is that he seems to have fully come to terms with being criticized, or being met with skepticism for his seemingly outlandish ideas. He showed it privately that day in the White House in a room full of some of the most powerful and wealthy people in the country, and he's shown it publicly numerous other times.

For a lot of us, the prospect of receiving criticism—especially public criticism—is enough to keep us from putting ourselves out there. This is particularly relevant in the age of social media, where you don't have to be famous to be met with harsh words from faceless keyboard warriors. But not all critics are acting in bad faith; sometimes a friend, family member, boss, or co-worker has constructive criticism that might actually help us, even if it's tough to hear.

Proverbs is full of advice for how the wise respond to criticism.

Reprove a wise man, and he will love you. (Proverbs 9:8)

Whoever ignores instruction despises himself, but he who listens to reproof gains intelligence. (Proverbs 15:32)

Listen to advice and accept instruction, that you may gain wisdom in the future. (Proverbs 19:20)

The Bible is also clear that we should go out of our way to surround ourselves with people who are willing to give us wise counsel, even—and perhaps especially—when it's not what we want to hear. "Let a righteous man strike me," King David wrote in Psalm 141:5, "it is a kindness." He knew better than most that "Where there is no guidance, a people falls, but in an abundance of counselors there is safety" (Proverbs 11:14).

But the Bible points out that not all criticism is created equal. Proverbs encourages us to listen to "life-giving reproof," which is hardly the way I would describe most of what happens in the internet comment section or social media replies.

So it's probably worth shutting off the social feed and opening up our hearts to constructive feedback from people who actually care about us and want to spur us toward a deeper relationship with Christ. Pray that God will put good counselors in your life and soften your heart to receive healthy critiques that might otherwise make you defensive.

Politics, Pro Wrestling, and the Apostle Paul

Political television shows are mostly performance theater—WWE-like productions in which each character has a predetermined role to play when the cameras are rolling. Off camera, though, you never know what you're going to get.

Tucker Carlson, for instance, is one of the kindest and most decent people you could ever meet. He's obsessed with fly fishing and spends as much time as he can with his wife and dogs in a tiny town in Maine, with none of the big city trappings that most celebrities demand. On the other end of the political spectrum, I've always found Anderson Cooper to be kind and genuinely interested in people off the air.

Unfortunately, though, they are outliers. In my experience, most people who talk on camera for a living seem to think everyone else should just be thankful to be graced by their presence. They dominate every conversation and generally act as if the world revolves around them.

So as I drove through the bustling streets of Manhattan en route to be a guest on ABC's *The View*, I didn't exactly know what to expect—but I was wary.

I prefer not to have much interaction with the hosts before an interview. In the final days of the 2016 presidential campaign,

I watched CNN's Jake Tapper pal around with Trump's deputy campaign manager David Bossie off air, asking about his children and other personal things, only to flip a switch on air and ask a question about whether a parent should feel comfortable with their daughter being in the same room as Trump.

David handled the question fine, but it stuck with me because of the jarring contrast. It was hard not to feel like Tapper was just trying to soften him up before going in hard during the interview.

Once I arrived at *The View*'s recording studio, I stayed sequestered in a prototypical dressing room with a large, well-lit mirror and a black director's chair embroidered with *The View* logo. Once on set, the co-hosts were polite but didn't say much, and the interview itself was pretty benign: we laughed, I got some cheers, endured some jeers and boos, and lived to fight another day.

But as my wife and I were walking off set, co-host Joy Behar—arguably the most liberal and aggressively anti-Trump of the bunch—complimented me and expressed her appreciation for my willingness to come on the show at all. She said, though, that she did have one question: "What's a nice guy like you doing working for somebody like Donald Trump anyway?"

I laughed it off and told her that I probably wasn't as nice as she thought, but I also said that my personal experience working with President Trump had been positive. "Yeah, but you know what I mean," she said.

The more I've thought about that question, I do understand what she was getting at—not just with Trump, but for plenty of people I know and love. The real question is, how can you disagree with things that a person does, but still support them; or even hate some of their actions, but still love them?

The answer is actually quite simple when you really think about it:

It's easy—that's what I've been doing with myself my entire life! As Paul wrote in Romans 7:

> I do not understand my own actions. For I do not do what I want, but I do the very thing I hate...I have the desire to do what is right, but not the ability to carry it out. For I do not do the good I want, but the evil I do not want is what I keep on doing.

In spite of the countless number of times and ways I have messed up, I still love myself. I still give myself another chance. The amount of grace that I extend to myself without a second thought is only surpassed by the limitless grace I receive from an all-knowing God. And yet I rarely extend that grace to others, especially those with whom I disagree.

Could this be because I have not fully appreciated just how unworthy I am of receiving any grace whatsoever from the perfect, all-powerful creator of the universe? And yet, as David wrote in Psalm 103, "as far as the east is from the west, so far does he remove our transgressions from us."

A deeper understanding of—and a genuine sense of wonder for—God's grace in our everyday lives can totally shift our perspective. And the grace we offer to others can lead to conversations about the grace that's available to them through the cross of Jesus Christ:

"But to the one who does not work, but believes in Him who justifies the ungodly, his faith is credited as righteousness" (Romans 4:5).

I'm Surrounded

When my White House memoir was released, I experienced public scrutiny unlike anything I ever had before. I was typically behind the scenes at the White House, only occasionally doing television or radio appearances on behalf of the president. But when your name is on the cover of the book, it's kind of up to you to promote and defend it.

Moments before my first interview on *Good Morning America*, one of the production assistants pulled a cushion out from under me so that host George Stephanopoulos would appear taller than me on television, even though he's at least several inches shorter. Stephanopoulos then promptly asked me if I had been fired from the White House. On *The View* later that day I was vigorously booed by the crowd. That night, on *The Late Show*, host Stephen Colbert told me during the commercial break right before I walked out on stage that if his audience heckled or booed me, he would stop the segment and tell them "that's not how we treat our guests." I certainly appreciated that sentiment, but it also reminded me that in all likelihood I would, indeed, get heckled and booed.

The benefit of going through the attacks, negative reviews, and criticisms (some justified) surrounding my book was that by the end of the media blitz I genuinely no longer cared what people had to say about me—even if it was written on the pages of the world's largest newspapers and discussed on the most watched cable television programs. In that regard, it was a liberating experience.

During that time period, I had the same routine before every interview. I would put on headphones and listen over and over to "Surrounded" by Michael W. Smith. "It may look like I'm surrounded but I'm surrounded by You," the lyrics repeat throughout the song. I let these words penetrate my cluttered mind and clarify for myself that even though I was the only one sitting in the interview chair, I wasn't alone—no matter what was about to come at me, I could be relaxed in knowing that I was surrounded by God's presence.

I repeated those words to myself as well, because far too often we forget to speak truth to ourselves, especially in the midst of adversity. Our minds are constantly having a dialogue with us—a one-sided conversation that can be full of negativity, doubts, frustrations, and worries.

In Lamentations 3, the writer expresses a total lack of peace to the point that he had "forgotten what happiness is." But rather than letting that fester and allowing his thoughts and emotions to continue pulling him down, his response was to preach the truth to himself:

"But this I call to mind, and therefore I have hope: The steadfast love of the Lord never ceases; his mercies never come to an end; they are new every morning; great is your faithfulness. 'The Lord is my portion,' says my soul, 'therefore I will hope in him.'"

Another example of this can be found in Psalm 42. "My tears have been my food day and night," the psalmist writes in a particularly brutal visual. But again, instead of letting the negativity fester, he picked up the other side of the conversation. "Why, my soul, are you downcast? Why are you so disturbed within me? Put your hope in God, for I will yet praise him, my Savior and my God."

Don't let your mind run wild today. As Paul wrote in 2 Corinthians 10:5, "take every thought captive to obey Christ." Preach the truth to yourself.

Serpents, Doves, and the Red Hen

Want to find out who your real friends are; or who cares about politics too much for their own good; or who's intolerant of alternative viewpoints and differing opinions? Get a job in the White House. From that point forward, your boss's views, statements, and actions will be assigned to you, for better or worse, by everyone ranging from your family members and personal friends to perfect strangers and social media trolls.

Sometimes your job is a point of fascination. Other times it's a point of appreciation, even affection. And still other times your spouse's friends won't talk to them anymore, because how could they be married to a person as despicable as you?

In 2018, the White House press secretary was asked to leave a restaurant called the Red Hen, just because she worked for Trump. Reporters wrote stories about how young White House staffers were being shunned on dating apps and in the D.C. social scene. Former cabinet members and senior aides were rejected from the coveted jobs and board positions that typically awaited them. Even at the company where I became CEO, some team members expressed after actually getting to know me that they had once questioned whether to join the company because they assumed I was probably not a good person. How could I be?

This moment in American life is particularly fraught with political division and bigotry against people who hold certain views or opinions. But this dynamic is nothing new. During the first hotly contested presidential election in U.S. history between John Adams and eventual winner Thomas Jefferson, Adams was attacked for being "hermaphroditical," as in someone who "has both male and female reproductive organs."[3] Yikes.

But even outside of politics, rivalries and differences of opinion are ever-present aspects of our lives.

In Ephesians 4, Paul calls for unity in the church, urging Christians "to walk in a manner worthy of the calling to which you have been called, with all humility and gentleness, with patience, bearing with one another in love, eager to maintain the unity of the Spirit in the bond of peace." Part of "bearing with one another" is giving fellow believers the benefit of the doubt in times of disagreement.

When dealing with the world, Jesus warns in Matthew 10:16, "I am sending you out as sheep in the midst of wolves, so be wise as serpents and innocent as doves." In other words, we are vulnerable to attack, like sheep, but should be smart about how we move in the world. As innocent doves, we've got to keep our reputations clean and not give any justifiable reason for accusations. As wise serpents, we need to discern when to embrace the danger that comes with speaking boldly and when to avoid unproductive confrontation.

Ask God to give you the courage to take risks for the faith and the wisdom to know when to stand strong and when to disengage.

The Children Who Never Made It Home

At 2:19 p.m. on Wednesday, February 14, 2018, I was standing along the curved wall of the Oval Office, where the president was hosting a working session on driving investment into distressed communities.

Unbeknownst to us, at that exact moment, a nineteen-year-old gunman had just opened fire on students and staff members at Marjory Stoneman Douglas High School in Parkland, Florida. When the carnage finally came to an end, seventeen people had lost their lives in the deadliest high school massacre in U.S. history. When I returned to my desk after the Oval Office event, horrifying images of children frantically running out of the school had just started to hit our television screens.

I never considered this until I worked in the West Wing, but staff in the White House experience such events much the same as the general public. Lines of communication are opened up between the administration and law enforcement officials on the ground, and the president is briefed with whatever information is available at the time. We typically don't have real-time visibility on every crisis situation as it happens. During such events, the Situation Room circulates regular email updates, but most of them just include information from open source intelligence (OSINT), like news reports.

Staffers in the Homeland Security offices downstairs hustle to quickly gather whatever information they can, but most of us stand speechless in front of our TVs, watching in horror like millions of other Americans in homes and offices around the country.

We would later come to find out that a former student, who had previously threatened to carry out such an attack, had finally decided to do it.

The following morning, the president addressed the nation. I stood in the back of the room, just behind a line of press and television cameras, dozens of cables snaking around my feet, and watched him deliver lines that would overwhelm the emotions of most parents if they tried to say them out loud.

"No parent should ever have to fear for their sons and daughters when they kiss them goodbye in the morning," he said.

On the walk back to the Oval Office after he was done speaking, I lagged behind the rest of the group and was the last staffer still outside when the president turned around and saw me about twenty yards away.

"I'm going to Florida tomorrow," he said emphatically. "I don't care what they have to do…Go tell them right now that they better figure it out."

I nodded. "Yes, sir."

As I would come to find out, the Secret Service was trying to pump the brakes on the president visiting Parkland. They were hoping to give themselves a little more time to iron out the logistical and security details. The Secret Service are total pros, and the president treated them all with the utmost respect. But he would occasionally grow frustrated when he couldn't do what he wanted on short notice.

I walked over to the Secret Service office in the Eisenhower Executive Office Building and delivered the message. "He's adamant about going tomorrow," I told the agents on duty. "He said he doesn't care what has to be done, he just wants to be on a plane to Parkland tomorrow afternoon."

"Roger that," one of them replied. "We're on it." And they delivered, as they always did.

I've quietly watched the president meet with parents who lost children, wives whose husbands were killed in battle, and kids whose daddies will never come home again. In every instance, I had a tendency to pick one single person and focus on them. My mind would race about the impact the tragedy might have on them. I would picture young parents as retirees, still going to sleep each night with a picture on the nightstand of their precious child who never grew up. I'd imagine elementary-age children as young adults trying to find their way, straining to remember the father they lost so young.

Occasionally, someone on staff would wonder aloud, Why, God?

The implication was, of course, what's the point of this? Is there any purpose, or is it all senseless, meaningless suffering? Some might even wonder to themselves, if God controls everything and yet such bad things happen, how is God himself not bad?

From the foundation of time itself, God has orchestrated the course of history to reveal his redemption story for mankind. This included allowing sin to enter the world. But this of course is not the same as sinning himself, which he cannot do. As the disciple John wrote, "God is light, and in him is no darkness at all" (1 John 1:5).

So then, as Christians we do "not grieve as others do who have no hope" (1 Thessalonians 4:13). Instead, we can rest assured that there is a purpose in our suffering and grief, even when we cannot see it. God teaches us things in the suffering that we would not otherwise learn. As David wrote in Psalm 119:71, "It is good for me that I was afflicted, that I might learn your statutes."

When we lose something, we are given the opportunity to display to the world that Christ is worth more than what we lost.

With that perspective, no tragedy could ever be meaningless. Just consider the picture of Christ himself, who was literally appointed to die. Why? So that God could show "his love for us in that while we were still sinners, Christ died for us" (Romans 5:8). He had a plan all along. It wasn't meaningless. And so it is for each of us.

"So we do not lose heart. Though our outer self is wasting away, our inner self is being renewed day by day. For this light momentary affliction is preparing for us an eternal weight of glory beyond all comparison, as we look not to the things that are seen but to the things that are unseen. For the things that are seen are transient, but the things that are unseen are eternal" (2 Corinthians 4:16–18).

So in the midst of the worst, God is enough. And in the midst of the best, God is still better.

CHAPTER 5

The Journey: Purpose in Everyday Life

In early 2016 before I joined the Trump campaign, I founded a media company called Yellowhammer News, named after Alabama's state bird, and we were attracting millions of readers to our online hub. I was also hosting a daily radio show and syndicating a statewide radio news network.

That March, a source contacted me with a tip. They had a thumb drive to give me, which they believed would change the course of Alabama history. But I could only retrieve it if I was willing to meet behind an obscure Birmingham gas station at midnight.

As I drove up U.S. Highway 280, swerving in and out of the sparse, late-night traffic and making my way from suburban Birmingham toward the city's center, I thought about the events of the past year that had led to this moment.

For many months the hottest rumor in Alabama politics was that our seventy-seven-year-old governor was engaged in an extramarital affair with his top political advisor, who was over thirty years younger. At first the idea seemed so absurd I dismissed it as politically motivated nonsense.

The governor's advisor had expressed appreciation the year before when I criticized other media outlets for publishing tabloid-style stories on the affair rumors, which at the time were unsubstantiated. I told her that I thought the coverage by other outlets had been unethical.

But during the week prior to this midnight meeting, I had been in discussions with confidential sources who claimed to have secret audio recordings that would confirm the rumors—in explicit detail. I was still wary of publishing something of that nature, but the sources also alleged that taxpayer resources were being abused to facilitate and cover up the affair.

Ultimately, they believed the governor—a husband of fifty years, father, church deacon, dermatologist, and now the state's top executive—had allowed his once sterling character to be corroded by power. And despite being confronted by his wife and church leaders, he still showed no contrition, giving his mistress unfettered access to every part of his life.

As he walked down the center aisle of the Old House Chamber after delivering the State of the State address, she was by his side. When he was photographed at a swanky Washington, D.C., gala typically reserved for only governors and their spouses, she was his date. And when any meeting in the Capitol was concluded, she was always the last one left in the room with him. The frustration and anger simmered for months, but it was now boiling over.

I pulled behind the gas station to find my source waiting exactly where they said they would be. The episode felt like a dramatic scene out of a spy movie, complete with me hopping out of my black sedan, Ruger compact nine-millimeter pistol tucked in my waistband. Not a single word was spoken. My source handed me the thumb drive, and we both turned around, stepped back into our vehicles, and sped away. When I made it home fifteen minutes later, I plugged the drive into my computer, opened the file, and within a few minutes knew it would indeed change the course of Alabama's political history.

As it turns out, the governor's wife had grown suspicious of her husband. So while at their beach house one weekend, she hit "record" on her cell phone, set it down on a table, and went for a walk alone on the beach. The governor took advantage of his sudden alone time, calling his mistress and talking like a couple of high schoolers hiding their relationship from their parents, who just wouldn't understand the depths of their endless love. When the governor's wife returned, she had captured it all on audio recording.

In the coming months, I broke numerous other stories on the saga. The couple had a secret safe deposit box together, although to this day we don't know what they stashed in it. He'd sometimes ditch his security detail to meet her in complete privacy as state troopers were left desperately searching for the "lost" governor. He'd dispatched a state helicopter to retrieve his wallet from his home in north Alabama and fly it to him at his beach house. We dubbed that scandal "#WalletCopter," and the governor defiantly admitted to it by saying, "I'm the governor and I had to have money. I had to buy something to eat." A year later he resigned in disgrace, cutting a deal with prosecutors to avoid jail time after multiple charges were filed against him.

Most tragically, he lost his marriage.

One Saturday afternoon after his divorce but before he was removed from office, I called him on his cell phone. I know it was a Saturday because we were both watching college football—me at my suburban Birmingham home, him at the Governor's Mansion in Montgomery.

He was sick and had almost completely lost his voice, but he was in good spirits, in spite of the controversy swirling around him. I told him I was not calling about anything in particular, but just wanted to tell him I had been praying for him and his family.

We spoke for about ten minutes, but it was not until we got off the phone that I had a revelation.

While the rest of Alabama was engulfed in a typical college football weekend and likely surrounded by friends and family, the state's governor was home alone, estranged from his family and many of his friends, with a hardened heart and the prospect of living his golden years in relative isolation. And even after he lost everything, including the powerful office to which he had so violently clung, he returned to his dermatology practice and hired as his office manager, believe it or not, his former political advisor and mistress.

So how did a church deacon, husband of fifty years, and successful doctor, who unexpectedly rose to the state's highest office and became the most powerful politician in Alabama, throw it all away? I suspect it didn't happen all at once, but slowly, in small, seemingly insignificant decisions in his day-to-day life. A shortcut here, a compromise there, and at some point he woke up alone having lost everything he would have claimed for most of his life that he loved the most.

It's a cautionary tale about politics, for sure, but it's also a reminder that each seemingly insignificant moment of our day either brings us closer to or farther away from God's design for our lives, and that regardless of which direction we are moving, the sum total of those tiny decisions will ultimately take us farther than we realize in the moment.

Hitler's Stationery

Tucked into a corner of the CIA's headquarters is a small museum dedicated to the Office of Strategic Services (OSS), the World War II–era predecessor to the CIA. The museum is a treasure trove of espionage history, but one artifact always stuck out to me more than the others—so much so that I would periodically return to see it again.

At some point in the waning days of World War II, a young member of the OSS named Richard Helms became one of the first intelligence officers to get inside Adolf Hitler's mountaintop retreat, known as the Eagle's Nest, and came into possession of Hitler's personal stationery. On V-E Day, which marked the end of World War II in Europe, Helms pulled it out and penned a letter to his son, Dennis, who at the time was just a toddler.

> Dear Dennis, The man who might have written on this card once controlled Europe—three short years ago when you were born. Today he is dead, his memory despised, his country in ruins. He had a thirst for power, a low opinion of man as an individual, and a fear of intellectual honesty. He was a force for evil in the world. His passing, his defeat—a boon for mankind. But thousands died that it might be so. The price for ridding society of bad is always high. Love, Daddy.

Over a half-century later, the day after Osama bin Laden was killed in a CIA-led operation in Pakistan, Dennis Helms donated his dad's letter to the CIA Museum as an ever-present reminder that "the price of ridding society of bad is always high." I would get goose bumps every time I returned to read it again.

A psychological analysis of Hitler commissioned by the OSS during World War II described his obsession with lying as a tool to manipulate the masses. "People will believe a big lie sooner than a little one," the analysts wrote of Hitler's approach, "and if you repeat it frequently enough people will sooner or later believe it." Hitler's policy of lies propelled him into power and ultimately played a significant role in his ability to perpetrate mass genocide. The truth matters a lot more than you might think.[1]

On the south wall of the CIA lobby, the first director of Central Intelligence, Allen Dulles, insisted upon having John 8:32 etched into the stone: "And ye shall know the truth and the truth shall make you free." This is now the CIA's unofficial motto. And while the agency has not always lived up to Jesus' words, they remind everyone who walks by them that truth and freedom are inextricably linked.

When Jesus told the Jews assembled on the Mount of Olives that "the truth shall make you free," they responded by saying, "We are offspring of Abraham and have never been enslaved to anyone." In other words, We're already free! Doesn't that sound a lot like us? I'm an American! This is the Land of the Free and the Home of the Brave!

Jesus' reply should stop us all in our tracks: "Everyone who commits sin is a slave to sin." Though we can be proud of the freedom we enjoy in this country, each of us is still a sinner.

Praise God that the truth of the gospel represents ultimate freedom—from sin, from our past, from a life of burden and worry. Ask God to make his desires your desires today, to give you that ultimate freedom—freedom from the bondage of a sinful heart.

The Little Things

You have likely never heard of the National Geospatial-Intelligence Agency (NGA), but its team members give the United States an extraordinary advantage over our adversaries.

The NGA collects, analyzes, and presents satellite images, maps, and other geospatial information to answer important questions like "Where am I? Where are the friendlies? Where are the enemies? When might they move? Where are the obstacles, natural or man-made, and how do I navigate among them?"

Their contributions to U.S. national security are immense, but one of their biggest contributions of all is also among their smallest—they design and build fine-scale models. Quietly toiling away in what amounts to the world's most secretive hobby shop, NGA modelers build miniature weapons systems, entire sections of war-torn cities, embassies, terrorist hideouts, and everything in between—all accurate down to the most minute detail. Some of them joke that if they're building a model of your house, it probably won't be long before you have a really bad day.

On the main floor of the CIA's headquarters sits one of the NGA's most famous work products: a perfect scale model of Osama bin Laden's fortified compound in Abbottabad, Pakistan, in which one inch equals seven feet. CIA analysts and SEAL Team members obsessively studied every inch of the model and later used it to build a life-size version to practice the daring—and ultimately successful—mission to take out the world's most infamous terrorist.

But during the six weeks it took to construct the miniature model, the modelers did not even know what exactly they were building. Based on the building's security features they assumed it housed a high-value target and even speculated about which one. But until the modelers saw the walls of the compound on television when details of the raid flooded the news, they were totally unaware of the integral role they were playing in history.

It turns out the little things aren't so little after all. We are each stewards of the resources and responsibilities God has entrusted to us. The Bible speaks at length about this principle with regard to our finances, but it also applies to all of the seemingly insignificant moments that make up everyday life.

How we treat the small things is a test of character. Every time we are faithful in small ways, we shore up the foundation of our character. Every time we aren't, we chip away at it. Have you ever noticed that committing a sin once makes it a lot easier to commit again? A white lie here, a cut corner there, and before long even when we feel convicted we think, *Well, I've already done it, so what's the use in fighting it now?*

The International Children's Bible translation of Proverbs 4:23 says, "Be very careful about what you think. Your thoughts run your life." So when Luke writes that "one who is faithful in a very little is also faithful in much, and one who is dishonest in a very little is also dishonest in much," we should consider the significance of even the smallest wayward thought.

The NGA modelers take pride in never cutting a corner, perfectly crafting and placing every structure, section of razor wire, or shrub, no matter how seemingly insignificant. Pray that God would shine a light on the small, dark corners of your heart that you have not fully surrendered to him, and approach today with a renewed appreciation for the enormous significance of small thoughts and actions, even when it's not apparent in the moment where they will lead or how they fit into his plan for your life.

The President's Time

The presidency is like an iceberg. The parts you see—the speeches, the ceremonial duties, the interviews, the walks out to Marine One, the photo ops before or after meetings—are like the tip of the iceberg sticking out of the water. The other 90 percent of the job exists out of sight in the murky depths below. Intelligence briefings, policy briefings, legislative strategy briefings—briefings, briefings, and more briefings. And mountains of paperwork.

A scheduler devotes the entire workday to ensuring the president's every waking hour is organized and maximized, and dozens of aides meticulously plan for every presidential meeting or movement. The reason for this is simple: the single most valuable commodity you have in the White House is the president's time. Some of the most vigorous debates in the West Wing are over which events or meetings get added to the president's schedule and which ones don't. If you want to know what a president and the current administration really care about, don't listen to what they say, just look at the president's schedule.

When the president leaves the White House, every step is planned out in advance by the White House Travel Office. If you're a member of the president's traveling staff, you receive a "trip book" that includes a minute-by-minute schedule, a vehicle manifest for who is riding in which van, helicopter, or airplane, descriptions of anyone the president will interact with, and even a weather forecast.

An intercom on Air Force One constantly updates staff on the president's ETA when he's arriving via helicopter: "The president is four minutes out...The president is one minute out... The president has arrived." The moment the president climbs aboard and sits down, the plane immediately begins to taxi for takeoff. I did not realize this the first time I flew on Air Force One, so when the pilot hit the throttle without any warning, my lunch slid off my desk and landed in my lap.

In short, the president of the United States never waits for anything. His time is just too valuable to waste even a single second.

So why do we approach our own time any differently? Sure, you're probably not going to have dozens of staffers planning your days and catering to your every need. But it is worth asking yourself, is my daily schedule worthy of the life I'm trying to build? If someone looked at your calendar, what would they say about your priorities—what is most important to you?

Moses' prayer in Psalm 90 shows us how we should approach the fleeting time we have in this life: "Teach us to number our days, that we may gain a heart of wisdom." Moses is not saying, life is short; live your best life now! Instead, he is saying to constantly remind yourself that this earthly life is short, but what comes next lasts forever. That realization—that wisdom—changes everything about how we spend our time. The bigger house, nicer car, and corner office promotion start to look a lot less obsession-worthy in the context of eternity.

As Paul writes in 2 Corinthians 4:18, "do not focus on what is seen, but on what is unseen. For what is seen is temporary, but what is unseen is eternal."

Pray for God to help you reject idleness, focus on things of eternal significance, and to spur your heart toward doing his will today.

The Kid Who Cut the White House Lawn

"Dear Mr. President: It would be my honor to mow the White House lawn some weekend for you... Here's a list of what I have and you are free to pick whatever you want: power mower, push mower, and weed whacker. I can bring extra fuel for the power mower and charged batteries for the weed whacker. I will do this at no charge."

After typing out the letter, the ten-year-old signed it "Frank," but his first attempt didn't go as well as he'd hoped, so he scratched it out and produced a more satisfactory signature in his second attempt.

When this letter made its way to my desk in the West Wing, I knew immediately that this kid had to cut the grass in the Rose Garden, but I had to figure out an angle. After a little brainstorming, I realized that the first week of August was being dubbed "American Dream Week" at the White House, which happened to coincide with Frank's eleventh birthday. The stars were aligning for our budding entrepreneur.

The resulting images of young Frank Giaccio mowing the Rose Garden lawn with such focus that he didn't even take a break when the president came out to greet him were some of the most lighthearted of the early days of the Trump administration. They were so good, in fact, that Frank's picture hung in a gilded frame in the East Wing of the White House for months afterward.

Reporters would sometimes ask why most of the letters we read at the beginning of press briefings were from kids. For one, their letters were usually funny or heartfelt and made for an interesting story. But kids also seemed a lot more willing to just flat-out ask for stuff. Can I cut the White House lawn? Sure. Can I bake cookies with the First Lady in the White House kitchen? Come on over. Can I spend the night in the White House? Okay, we stopped short of that one. But you get the idea. And there's something to learn from that.

In Luke 11:9–13, Jesus implores us, "Ask, and it will be given to you . . . For everyone who asks receives . . . If you then, who are evil, know how to give good gifts to your children, how much more will the heavenly Father give the Holy Spirit to those who ask him!"

So why are we not asking our heavenly Father for good gifts? One reason, perhaps, is that we're not fully embracing everything Jesus means when he tells us we have to become like children (Matthew 18:3–4). When I think about my own child, a six-year-old little boy named Shep, he will ask me for just about anything you could imagine, but is also generally content (albeit with some occasional whining) if the answer is no.

Can we fly on a rocket ship, Daddy? I don't think so, buddy. Can I get another monster truck at the toy store? Not right now. Can I have some candy? Maybe later. Can I drive the car, please? No chance.

Children are so good at asking, and also mostly accepting (even if begrudgingly) that their parents are only going to give them what's actually in their best interest. We would benefit from adopting a similar posture (minus the begrudging part) in prayer, knowing that the God of the universe knows infinitely well what is for our good and for his glory.

This isn't a call to "name it and claim it" or treat God like he's our Santa Claus in the sky, granting us all of our material wishes. Prayer is the God-designed mechanism for us to build a deeper relationship with him. So when Jesus says in John 15:7, "If you abide in me, and my words abide in you, ask whatever you wish, and it will be done for you," we would do better to focus on the first half of that sentence. Abiding is all about building a relationship through which God actually changes the sinful desires of our hearts to be more in line with his own. And if our desires are in line with God's desires, we are far more likely to be asking him for things that he actually wants to give us—even massive, mountain-moving things.

As C. S. Lewis wrote:

It would seem that Our Lord finds our desires not too strong, but too weak. We are half-hearted creatures, fooling about with drink and sex and ambition when infinite joy is offered us, like an ignorant child who wants to go on making mud pies in a slum because he cannot imagine what is meant by the offer of a holiday at the sea. We are far too easily pleased.

What do the things you're currently asking God for say about the desires of your heart?

Prayers Up on the Osprey

Traveling with the president was perhaps the most eye-opening experience of my early days in the White House. I had never considered the logistical achievement required to safely move him and his staff around the world. Every potential threat must be taken into account. Giant military cargo planes transported the presidential limousine—"The Beast"—everywhere we went. The well-dressed Secret Service agents wearing their shades were ever present at his side, but rarely seen were the Counter Assault Teams decked out in tactical gear, ready to meet any threat with overwhelming force. The press had to be accounted for, too. They had a dedicated cabin aboard Air Force One at the back of the plane, and vans were provided to them as part of the presidential motorcade.

With every step carefully planned, every route cleared in advance, and every flight always number one for departure, every trip took a fraction of the time it would if we were flying commercial. Needless to say, post–White House treks through traffic jams and TSA lines were an unwelcome return to reality.

But there was one particular aspect of traveling with the president that was unlike anything else I had experienced before: flying in an MV-22 Osprey, the tilt-rotor transport aircraft that combines the vertical takeoff and landing capabilities of a helicopter with the speed of a turboprop airplane. During trips when Air Force One would land too far from our destination to complete the trip via motorcade, the president would board Marine One and the rest of us would run up the open bay door of an Osprey, pile into its jump seats, and hold on for dear life.

The back bay door would never fully close, often leaving a member of the flight crew casually sitting there (hopefully tethered in) peering over the edge, inches away from tumbling out. I've flown in airplanes through intense turbulence numerous times and can sleep right through it. But I never quite got comfortable on the Ospreys, even though the Marines flying them always got us where we were going smoothly and safely.

Every time we were about to take off in one, I would feel compelled to say a prayer—to ask God's forgiveness for whatever I'd done wrong that day in anticipation of the worst, and then petition for an uneventful, safe flight. It wouldn't quite devolve into a classic "Get me out of this alive and I promise to never do anything wrong again!" type prayer. But you get the idea.

This may seem silly and ridiculous, but we often treat our prayer life this way—asking for things only in times of trouble. There's nothing wrong with saying a prayer at any moment. 1 Thessalonians 5:17 implores us to "pray without ceasing." 1 Peter 5:7 says to "cast all your anxieties on him, because he cares for you." But there is something revealing about the guilt-ridden impulse to say a prayer in times of stress, in the hope that God will begrudgingly come to the rescue or shower his blessings upon us. It completely misses the point of prayer: our all-powerful, all-knowing God actually wants a relationship with us.

Our habits (like always saying a prayer right before takeoff) do not change God's love for us. Instead, God's love for us should change our habits. We should not pray in some misguided, perhaps even subconscious attempt to increase God's love for us. We should pray because God's love for us is irresistible, drawing us ever closer to him, into a deeper and deeper relationship with a God who wants to give us every good gift. In short, spiritual disciplines like prayer are not about earning God's love; they're about enjoying it.

"Delight yourself in the LORD, and he will give you the desires of your heart" (Psalm 37:4).

The President's Red Button

The first time you enter the Oval Office, it's hard not to be overwhelmed by it all.

There's the grandfather clock built in the late 1700s that's sat beside the entryway door counting the seconds of history for decades. There's the ornate ceiling medallion installed in 1934 that features a bald eagle encircled by an unusual array of eight-pointed stars. There's the way the doors almost seamlessly disappear into the walls. There's the surreal ambiance of a room with curved walls, so well lit that there don't seem to be any shadows. There are the historical paintings of legendary Americans like Washington and Jefferson, or the busts of icons like MLK or Winston Churchill.

And then there's the desk, arguably the most iconic piece of all. It was ornately carved out of English oak timbers from the HMS Resolute and had been given by Queen Victoria to President Rutherford B. Hayes in 1880. Presidents Kennedy, Reagan, Clinton, Bush, and Obama all used the desk in the Oval Office, and it combined the two things Trump appreciated most in White House furniture: history and luxury.

But there was one curiosity that inevitably attracted the attention of first-time guests. On top of the desk, in addition to multiple phone systems and the stacks of paperwork Trump would often keep piled high, sat a small wooden box, approximately nine inches long and three inches wide. A golden presidential seal was imprinted on top of it, right in the middle, and a small red button about the size of a dime could be seen beside the seal.

What happens if he presses that red button? I'm sure many first-time visitors wondered to themselves.

If Trump noticed someone glancing at the box—and sometimes completely unprompted—he would pick it up and move it farther away from himself. "Don't worry about that," he'd say. "No one wants me to push that button, so we'll just keep it over here. Now, what were you saying?"

Guests would laugh nervously, and the conversation would continue, until several minutes later Trump would suddenly move it closer to himself without actually saying anything about it. Then, later in the conversation, out of nowhere, he'd suddenly press the button. Guests would freeze. Then, not sure what to do, they would look at one another with raised eyebrows. Did we just go to war? Is some adversarial nation's capital minutes away from being turned into a radioactive parking lot?

Moments later, the door would swing open and a steward would enter the room carrying a silver platter that held a glass filled with Diet Coke, and Trump would burst out laughing. "That red button!" he'd exclaim. "People never know what to think about the red button! Is he launching the nukes?!" Most guests would double over laughing at the prankster in chief.

When listing the character traits of God, I doubt many people think to throw in "great sense of humor," and so you may be surprised to hear that God is actually the most hilarious being in the entire universe. As Paul wrote in Colossians 1:18, God is "preeminent" in "everything," and that includes humor. After all, he put hundreds of tiny legs on a millipede. He made parrots repeat the things they hear. When he created seahorses, it's like he thought to himself, what if I made a miniature saxophone that swims in the ocean? And then he actually did it!

The devil doesn't want you to laugh with a pure heart. He wants you to be preoccupied and consumed by his perversions of fun that can rob God's people of true joy. As the fictitious high-ranking demon said in C. S. Lewis' *The Screwtape Letters*, "Fun is closely related to Joy…It promotes charity, courage, contentment and many other evils." In other words, Satan weaponizes fun; he doesn't enjoy it.

When we think about Jesus, our minds often—and rightly—picture a God who gave his life for us. We remember Isaiah 53's prophecy of a savior "despised and rejected by men, a man of sorrows and acquainted with grief." But let's also remember, that was only for a short time—and so it will be for us, "for this light momentary affliction is preparing for us an eternal weight of glory beyond all comparison" (2 Corinthians 4:17).

Luke 6:21 promises, "Blessed are you who weep now, for you shall laugh."

Revelation 21:4 envisions an inevitable future when "He will wipe away every tear from their eyes, and death shall be no more, neither shall there be mourning, nor crying, nor pain anymore, for the former things have passed away."

Crying will end. Pain will end. But laughter will never end. What a wonderful thought, and a reminder that every pure laugh in this life is a tiny glimpse of eternity with the God of good humor.

Briefing Rooms and Lions' Dens

White House press secretary is arguably the toughest job in government. You're communicating on behalf of someone else, so the thoughts, positions, and statements are not always your own. You're expected to speak with authority about every subject under the sun, almost none of which are your area of expertise. Every journalist in the room is trying to craft questions in the way that's most likely to trip you up or expose some hypocrisy, inconsistency, or divide inside the administration. And you're doing it all every day on live television. Oh, and your mistakes get played on a loop on cable news so all of your friends and colleagues watch you mess up over and over again, as does the most powerful person on the planet, who's particularly disappointed in your performance.

Part of my job in the White House was to help then–press secretary Sarah Sanders prepare to brief every day. A team of researchers and press aides would begin early in the morning compiling the day's hot-button issues and responses to anticipated lines of questioning. Subject matter experts were brought in to brief her on topics ranging from national security to tax policy to disaster relief. A "briefing book" was built throughout the day with tabs she could flip to as a reporter began asking about a given topic. And then about half a dozen of us would aggressively pepper her with questions to simulate the high-pressure environment as much as possible.

Sarah had a routine. Briefing prep dominated the morning. Before going out, she would speak to the president to get his input and direction. Then she would go into her office alone, shut the door, and spend time reading a devotion and praying. Every single time, every single day. The rest of the day Sarah's office was a nonstop revolving door of activity. But that time right before the briefing was the only moment when everyone knew to leave her alone and not interrupt.

One of the most important things any of us can do is intentionally build into our daily lives a regular, recurring encounter with God. The prophet Daniel, who was an advisor to four kings, modeled this for us in the Old Testament when he "got down on his knees three times a day and prayed and gave thanks before his God" (Daniel 6:10).

So when the most perilous moment of Daniel's life came—when the king ordered him to be thrown into a den of lions—he was not reduced to panic; his daily encounters with God gave him the strength and peace he needed not only to survive, but to thrive in the face of adversity and to display God's glory to everyone he encountered, including the king.

The morning after he threw Daniel in the lion's den—and spent a sleepless night regretting it—he rushed over and called out, "O Daniel, servant of the living God, has your God, whom you serve continually, been able to deliver you from the lions?" And Daniel replied, "My God sent his angel and shut the lions' mouths, and they have not harmed me, because I was found blameless."

We all have to face the metaphorical lions, just maybe not as publicly as the White House press secretary. If we're going to be prepared when the moment comes, it starts with spiritual discipline long before the trial.

Space Station, This Is Your President Speaking

In the midst of the alphabet soup of my White House email inbox, one particular acronym stuck out: NASA. When you're sitting in the West Wing and someone you don't know from a government agency reaches out, there's a decent chance something is on fire and is about to derail your day. So when I quickly opened the email from NASA's head of communications, I was relieved to see that we didn't have a budding catastrophe on our hands.

In fact, she had what would turn out to be a pretty interesting request.

Astronaut Peggy Whitson was currently aboard the International Space Station and poised to break the record for the most cumulative time spent in space. NASA wanted to know if the president might participate in some type of event celebrating this historic milestone. I immediately had an idea, so I picked up the phone at my desk and called them.

"I've seen past presidents call the space station before; could he do that?" I asked.

"Oh, yes," NASA's comms chief replied, clearly excited. "We could set up a videoconference anywhere you want and broadcast it live."

"The Oval Office?" I asked.

"Yes, of course, that would be amazing," she said.

The next day, standing on the patio just off the Oval Office, I asked the president if he were interested in doing the call. He was over the moon about it, launching into a wistful thought stream about how the space race captured people's imaginations and inspired an entire generation. The space station call was definitely on.

Over the next few weeks, I witnessed firsthand the thorough precision that NASA is known for. Their engineers drew detailed, scale diagrams of the Oval Office with all of the production equipment positioned where it would be. I got a crash course in orbital mechanics and how the live communications would work. We went into the Oval and did a walk-through of exactly how it would all play out. And we coordinated with NASA's spaceflight team to pinpoint the exact time the call would need to take place.

On the day of the event, there was a buzz of excitement in the Oval suite. For staff, this was one of those how cool is this? moments. Ultimately, all of the preparation paid off. When the connection was made flawlessly between the space station, Mission Control in Houston, and the White House, the president couldn't help but smile.

"That's what we like," he said, as an audience of millions watched from around the world. "Great American equipment that works, and this isn't easy."

He's right about that. The scientific understanding and technological capabilities required to make that routine call between Earth and space boggle the mind. Most of us float through life without having to give much thought to the scientific wonders that surround us. And most conversations about science these days are so politicized that it seems impossible to ascertain the truth, especially when you're being attacked by people yelling that you're a "science denier" and should just "trust the science!"

In reality, the most foundational truths about science are even more controversial than any heterodox views on climate change, mRNA vaccines, or COVID origins:

Science and the Christian faith are perfectly congruent.

Every scientific discovery proclaims the glory of God.

Every shred of scientific evidence points to our Creator. Just consider these facts:

At the moment the universe began, if gravity had been any weaker, it would not have been able to form planets and galaxies, and stars wouldn't have been hot enough for nuclear fusion. But if gravity had been any stronger, the entire universe would have collapsed on itself and stars would have burned too hot, too fast to ever create the environment needed for life to exist. On top of that, our planet just happens to be in exactly the right place, with just the right size sun, which is just the right age and emits just the right amount of light—and we're orbiting it just right, with unfathomably exact precision, to make life sustainable. In other words the universe is so fine-tuned that it defies logic to guess that it happened by some happy accident.

"The heavens declare the glory of God, and the sky above proclaims his handiwork" (Psalm 19:1).

On the opposite end of the scale spectrum, modern science has found microscopic organisms so tiny and complex that Charles Darwin himself conceded before his death that if they were ever to be discovered, his theory of evolution would "absolutely break down."[2] Philosophies that deny supernatural, intelligent design have failed to explain how genetic information—the DNA coiled into each of the trillions of cells in each body—ever got into biological matter in the first place.

And perhaps most profoundly of all, how do we explain human consciousness? If it's impossible for something to come from nothing, then how did the universe go from dead matter with no life, no thinking and no feeling, to you having the capacity to understand and assess these words, even as you effortlessly perceive the world around you through each of your senses? Unless, of course, it didn't. Unless it all—including our very consciousness—really began with the mind of the Creator.

"Then the Lord God formed the man of dust from the ground and breathed into his nostrils the breath of life, and the man became a living creature" (Genesis 2:7).

As Lee Strobel, an atheist investigative journalist who set out to disprove Christ, realized:

When I opened my mind to the possibility of an explanation beyond naturalism, the theory denying any supernatural existence in the universe, I found that the design hypothesis—that says there is a purposeful, intelligent, created order to the universe—most clearly accounted for the evidence of science.

So yeah, trust the science.[3]

Chapter 6

The Collision: Faith and Politics

For Such a Time as This?

In the fall of 2022, just ahead of contentious midterm elections around the United States, I was scrolling through Twitter when a video caught my eye. A political commentator and former White House colleague of mine was delivering an impassioned speech, urging listeners to go to the polls and vote for Republican candidates. The rhetoric was pretty typical of what you'd expect at any political rally; but my ears perked up when she quoted scripture, declaring that listeners in the assembled crowd had been put there "for such a time as this"—to vote in the 2022 midterm elections. This, too, was not that abnormal, and I generally agreed with the sentiment and sense of urgency. This was an important election, and voting Republican was what I planned to do—and I hoped others would as well.

But that remark—a reference to Esther 4, in which Mordecai urges Queen Esther to use her royal position to influence the king and save God's people from his wrath—didn't sit right with me. I couldn't quite put my finger on why it bothered me at first. After all, the context of the scripture is political. Mordecai, who saved the king from an assassination plot and would become his chief advisor, was using his political influence to urge the queen to use her political influence to change the king's policies toward the Jews. That's some serious palace intrigue—about as political as it gets!

So I thought, *Maybe I'm unfairly judging the message because of the messenger.* While in the White House, she had never shown any evidence of being a believer. At one point, when I apologized to her for a confrontation we had in front of our colleagues and noted that I felt particularly bad because our pastor had just preached on how to handle disagreements, she was not particularly interested and noted that she'd never spent much time reading the Bible.

The more I thought about it, though, the more I zeroed in on the real reason for my discomfort with her "for such a time as this" rhetoric. The implication was not just that Christians should participate in the political process and let our faith guide the decisions we make when exercising our right to vote. No, the implication was that God had put American Christians here at this moment in history for the sole purpose of voting in an election, as if politics is the central focus of our entire lives and the only hope for our salvation. Essentially, you were put on this Earth to save America from Democrats.

I just don't believe that's true, and I say that having devoted much of my adult life to advancing various conservative principles, priorities, candidates, and causes. I also say that while simultaneously believing in the virtue of fighting tooth and nail to preserve the values, culture, and government policies that align most closely with God's vision for justice, righteousness, and human flourishing.

This is an oversimplification, but it seems like American Christians now fall into one of two camps when it comes to political engagement.

There are the timid Christians who seem to think that other Christians who push back against the evil in our cultural and political forces arrayed against our beliefs should stop being mean and learn to turn the other cheek. You'll find the analysis of this first group of Christians in the pages of the *New York Times* opinion section, pointing out everything that's wrong with "evangelicals." Or you'll see members from this group wringing their hands on the set of MSNBC shows. Their public commentary and virtue signaling mostly follows along with whatever the liberal media says is the most important topic in society at the time—the "current thing," as I like to call it. I find many in this camp to be condescending and their air of superiority—as if they are the only "true" Christians left—off-putting.

And I can't help but wonder if they've ever asked themselves, Why do leftist media outlets—the ones whose talking heads despise everything Christians believe—continue to invite me on and praise what I'm saying? It's like the late-career Republican politicians who once had their reputations destroyed by mainstream media, but who later, once they're no longer as relevant, bask in the media love fest, slam conservatives, and pine for a bygone era of bipartisan cooperation that never really existed.

Then there are the ends-justify-the-means Christians who live their lives in a perpetual state of all-out hostility against anyone they perceive to be a threat to…you name it…American culture, western civilization, our way of life, or whatever term you want to use. You can follow this group of Christians as they wage war on social media, often garnering millions of followers along the way, and you'll find their views in the most popular platforms and publications of the "new right." They're always fighting fire with fire, being much more inclined to defend the Christian faith than to model it.

As you could probably guess, this second group includes at times, well…me, at least much more than the first. And it certainly includes many more of my friends than the first. So I have to admit that we have often been guilty of letting politics rise way too high in our life's hierarchy of priorities, and of justifying our ruthlessness by simply pointing to the perceived severity of the threat.

I cringe to think that I'm sometimes the walking embodiment of Proverbs 14:12: "There is a way that seems right to a man, but its end is the way to death." I'm also reminded of when God told Moses to "tell the rock" to "yield its water" so that God's people could drink, and Moses instead "struck the rock with his staff" (Numbers 20). The water came out all the same, and God's people drank, but because Moses disobeyed God's instructions—striking the rock instead of speaking to it—he did not get to enter the Promised Land. Clearly, then, using any means necessary to reach an end—no matter how desirable that end might be—is not an acceptable approach to a righteous God.

So I'd submit that several things can be true at once:

Bringing people to the saving knowledge of Jesus Christ is of supreme importance—yes, even more important than winning any political fight;

Aggressively advocating for government policies that preserve our freedoms and most closely reflect the Judeo-Christian tradition on which our country was founded is a noble pursuit; and

Supporting the flawed politicians who defend and advance those policies is not automatically heretical, nor is it tacit approval of all of their actions.

So where should electoral politics fit into our lives? What does the Bible say about how we should engage in the political process, or for whom we should vote—or whether we should vote at all? What role should faith play in the public square, and should political and cultural events of the day influence what's preached from the pulpit? How should Christians live in a world that has been consumed by politics, much less worship in churches being torn apart by political factions?

I'll get to all of that. But as a general foundation—and as a reminder of what truly matters the most—I believe C. S. Lewis had it exactly right in *Mere Christianity*:

> If individuals live only seventy years, then a state, or a nation, or a civilization, which may last for a thousand years, is more important than an individual. But if Christianity is true, then the individual is not only more important but incomparably more important, for he is everlasting and the life of a state or a civilization, compared with his, is only a moment.

The Gospel and the Ballot Box

The first conversation I ever had with Donald Trump took place during a live radio interview in the summer of 2015, and during that interview we started talking about faith. Trump was promising to deliver for Christians on the policy issues we cared about.

"There's an assault on anything having to do with Christianity," he told me. "I will go so strongly against so many of these things."

Once elected, that is exactly what he did. He put pro-life justices on the Supreme Court, ultimately resulting in *Roe v. Wade* being overturned. He instructed the IRS to never threaten to revoke the tax-exempt status of churches and faith-based nonprofits if their leaders spoke out on moral or political issues. He directed all federal agencies to preserve their employees' religious liberty and not require them to take certain actions that would go against their sincerely held beliefs. He exempted religious organizations from Obamacare's contraception mandate. He ended federal funding for international organizations involved in abortions. He ended the Obama-era transgender policy in public schools, no longer allowing biological males to go into girls' bathrooms and locker rooms. The list could go on and on.

"There was a recent poll where the evangelicals said that I was their number-one choice," Trump had boasted in my 2015 conversation with him. And, boy, was he proven right on that. He ultimately received overwhelming—perhaps even record-breaking—support from evangelicals. I was one of them. But I also had Christian friends and family members—people I love and whose opinion I respect—who thought my support of Trump was misguided, at best.

I would tell them privately the same thing that I have said in numerous TV and radio interviews over the years: Trump (the man) is not the best example of the Christian faith, but Trump (the president and politician) has been a great defender of it from a policy perspective. And I will be forever grateful for the countless unborn children whose lives he saved by implementing the most sweeping pro-life presidency in history.

I would also sometimes tell them the story of my Christian friends in Egypt, where I have spent a good bit of time.

In 2013, Egyptians took to the streets by the millions to protest the Islamist government of Mohamed Morsi of the Muslim Brotherhood. They supported the rise of military general Abdel Fattah el-Sisi, who wanted to crush ISIS in the Sinai and promised Christians—and other religious minorities—greater civic equality. El-Sisi wasn't George Washington, though. He wasn't going to rise to power, only to give it back to the people in an act of democratic heroism. He would still control a largely authoritarian, militarized state. And he was a devout Muslim. In short, he was far from everything Christians wanted. But he was far better than the alternative, and so they campaigned hard for him. In fact, one of my Christian friends still had a homemade campaign poster for him in their bedroom several years after he came to power.

When some American Christians demean their Trump-supporting brothers and sisters for lacking moral courage, I've often thought of Egypt.

What about Egyptian Christians, whose churches were bombed and whose dead bodies were paraded through the streets while you flaunted your moral superiority on Twitter from the comfort of your couch? Did they lack moral courage, as well, for supporting a Muslim authoritarian over an Islamist who wanted the streets to run red with their blood?

But no matter how strongly I personally feel about that, or how confident I am in my principled justification for voting for—and ultimately working for—Trump, I also respect the principled decision of other Christians to either oppose Trump or abstain from voting at all.

This is where any Christian should begin when wrestling with how to faithfully engage in politics, especially at this contentious and divided moment in American life: grace. No matter how much clarity and conviction we have in the decisions we make to support certain candidates, we have to find it within ourselves to offer grace to fellow believers who looked at the same facts, weighed the same pros and cons, and ultimately landed in a different place than we did.

The fact is, there is no Biblical mandate to vote or to be engaged in the political process at all, at least in part because the concept of representative democracy was unheard of in Biblical times. But scripture does give us Biblical principles that are clearly applicable to the political decisions we're facing today.

The first foundational principle is that God is the ultimate ruler, no matter who rules on Earth. And no matter if it rubs our freedom-loving, American sensibilities the wrong way, God doesn't rule over a democracy—he is the supreme, all powerful king and we are his subjects. Psalm 47:7 says, "God is the King of all the earth." And Revelation 19:16 says, "On his robe and on his thigh he has a name written, King of kings and Lord of lords."

Second, God "created man in his own image" (Genesis 1:27) and uniquely empowered us among all of his Creation to rule the world, an extraordinary privilege and responsibility. "You have given him dominion over the works of your hands; you have put all things under his feet," the Psalmist says (Psalm 8:6).

Third, in ruling here on Earth, we are to be a reflection of God's just rule over everything. Of course, we know that even the most godly ruler will fall short of being a perfect reflection of God's rule, because "all have sinned and fall short of the glory of God" (Romans 3:23). But God has entrusted those who govern on Earth to administer justice on his behalf—to encourage human flourishing, protect the unalienable, God-given rights of every person equally, and punish those who do wrong. He has sent "governors...to punish those who do evil and to praise those who do good" (1 Peter 2:14).

Fourth and finally, those who govern on Earth are responsible to God and will be held accountable by him. Even King David, whom God called "a man after my heart, who will do all my will" (Acts 13:22), lost a son as a result of his sin.

Now, you may be reading these principles and thinking, Even if I agree with all of this, how does any of it apply to me? I'm not a government official, much less a king. The fact is, these principles take on a particularly relevant meaning for all of us who live in a representative republic, where ultimate power lies with the people, because we are both the governed and the governor. Even if we do not hold public office, our system of government empowers us to select leaders who will reflect God's rule and administer his justice.

So while there is no Biblical mandate to vote, scripture calls us to use our political power to reflect God's rule and justice here on Earth, and makes it clear that we will be held accountable for the choices we make—whether that choice is to vote one way or another, or to make the intentional decision not to vote at all.

Politics in the Church

In the summer of 2019, I was sitting in my company's headquarters in downtown Birmingham, Alabama, purposefully—and blissfully—ignorant of the day-to-day political machinations going on in Washington, D.C. I had left my White House job, published my memoir, and hadn't yet been asked to rejoin the Trump administration in the Office of the Director of National Intelligence. As I leaned back in my chair and propped up a foot on the office's exposed brick wall, my phone lit up with a familiar name: David Platt.

In 2006, at the age of twenty-six, David had become known as "the youngest megachurch pastor in the United States" when he was named the senior pastor of the Church at Brook Hills in Birmingham. In 2010, he became one of the most famous pastors in the country when he published his first book, *Radical*, which went on to sell more than a million copies. We first met in 2012, when my wife, Megan, and I moved to Birmingham and David became our pastor. Megan later joined the Brook Hills staff in a communications role.

Since that time, both David's life and mine had taken several unexpected turns, diverging and converging along the way. In February of 2017, a month after I went to work in the White House, David unexpectedly became our pastor for a second time at McLean Bible Church in suburban Washington, D.C. We joked that it was a little creepy for him, Heather, and their kids to be following Megan and me around the country, but we were glad to have them along for the ride nonetheless.

Now back in Alabama, I answered the phone and asked David if he was calling to let me know that he and his family were moving back as well. He laughed, but it was quickly apparent that he wasn't calling just to catch up. "Have you seen the news?" he asked. I sat up in my chair and googled "David Platt" on my laptop as I briefly explained how unplugged I was from most of what was happening in the world. I immediately saw why he was calling, as he began to explain.

The day before, just after David had finished preaching and briefly stepped backstage, he was shocked to learn from a White House official that the presidential motorcade was about to pull up at the church and President Trump was hoping that the congregation—and David—would pray for him.

Moments later David was on stage with the president of the United States, placing his hand on the president's back and praying that God would give him grace, wisdom, and mercy; that Trump would trust in and lean on God; that he would make just and righteous decisions. I watched a video of their interaction on mute as David explained the situation, and I was struck by Trump's body language. I've never been in a room with Trump that he didn't dominate, or witnessed a conversation that he didn't lead and control. But in that moment he was subdued, quietly taking it all in. When the prayer was over, Trump mouthed "amen" and didn't even seek to speak to the congregation of thousands. He politely shook David's hand, waved to the congregation, and walked off the stage.

But David wasn't calling just to recount this surreal experience. He had set off a firestorm, both within his congregation and in the press. He was hoping I could use my experience dealing with the national media to help him navigate the unexpected deluge of stories being written by mainstream outlets, especially the *Washington Post*. Trump, the church, and controversy: as it turns out, that's a recipe for a wild news cycle in both the mainstream and faith-based media.

I spoke to reporters from numerous mainstream news outlets, and their cynicism was palpable as I tried to help them understand David's complete lack of political motivation or desire to cozy up to power. It was like they couldn't believe anyone in the nation's capital wasn't a political animal. A megachurch pastor? Psshhh, he's probably more opportunistic than the politicians!

I told several of them off the record that David had actually declined my invitation to speak at an Easter prayer breakfast we had tried to organize at the White House, eschewing the political spotlight for fear that it would (1) detract from his singular mission to spread the Gospel, and (2) spark division inside his church, which is one of the most diverse (politically, racially, socioeconomically, etc.) in the country.

The entire exercise was a reminder not only of the pervasive liberal bias and general ignorance—and skepticism—of Christianity that exists in the mainstream media but also of the bias toward conflict and controversy that exists in both mainstream and faith-based media.

As David wrestled with the sudden onslaught of attention and criticism from some church members who were offended by his decision to pray for Trump on stage, he decided to write a letter to his congregation explaining the Biblical reasoning behind his approach.

After describing the surprising circumstances leading up to Trump walking out on stage, David wrote that his "aim was in no way to endorse the president, his policies, or his party, but to obey God's command to pray for our president and other leaders to govern in the way [1 Timothy 2:1–6] portrays." He went on to lament the fact that some members of the church were "hurt that [he] made this decision" and expressed a desire to lead the church "with God's Word in a way that transcends political party and position." In conclusion he asked the church, "would you pray with me for the gospel seed that was sown today to bear fruit in the president's heart? Would you also pray with me that God will help us to guard the gospel in every way as we spread the gospel everywhere?"

Immediately, many of the people who were thrilled that David had prayed for President Trump were now upset that he felt the need to explain himself. "David Platt, McLean Bible Church pastor, apologizes for praying for Donald Trump," read a dishonest *Washington Times* headline that was emblematic of the new round of media blowback.[1]

For the next several years, McLean was embroiled in a seemingly never-ending wave of controversy, including lawsuits, hostile takeover attempts, and scurrilous blogging campaigns smearing

David as a "woke" pastor. The entire prolonged episode would have been comically absurd if it wasn't so effective in dividing one of America's great churches at exactly the moment its proximity to—and influence on—our nation's leaders was so needed.

Entire seminary courses could be devoted to unpacking and analyzing every twist and turn of the McLean saga—and they probably should be. But here's the foundational takeaway for all of us, whether we're pastors, lay leaders in the church, members, or visitors: Any of us who contribute to politics dividing the church are in the wrong, no matter how convinced we are that our political views are right.

There are primary issues that are non-negotiable in the church, like the divine, virgin birth of Jesus; his sinless life and his death, burial, and resurrection; the principle that we are saved by grace alone, through faith alone; the concept of the Trinity; the infallible nature of Scripture; and all the undeniable character traits of God, from his omniscience and omnipresence to his perfection and boundless power. These issues are inseparable from what it means to be a Christian.

Then there are secondary issues, like the mystery of God's sovereign foreknowledge and man's will and responsibility; the ideal type of church governance; whether women should be allowed to serve in church leadership; and the proper mode of baptism, just to name a few. These are issues that may divide denominations, but they should not divide the Church—with a capital "C"—or hinder our ability to work together toward our common purpose of spreading the Gospel to the nations.

Politics is, at best, a tertiary issue, a space in which disagreements and ethical debates can take place around dinner tables and water coolers, in social media comment sections, and sure, among church members, too. In fact, disagreements over secondary and tertiary matters can actually highlight the power of Christ who unites us, if handled appropriately. But even though we all have strong feelings on these issues of morality and conscience—deeply informed by our faith—allowing these things to divide us can only be described as one thing: sin.

"God is not a God of confusion but of peace," the Apostle Paul says (1 Corinthians 14:33). From the very beginning of Genesis, we see God bringing order to chaos. In Romans 5 we see our opportunity to "have peace with God through our Lord Jesus Christ." We are not talking about a superficial peace—one that is without conflict or just ignores differences. After all, ultimate peace was only made possible through history's greatest conflict. God was willing to sacrifice his only Son to create a pathway to reconciliation between us and him. Surely, then, we can find it within ourselves to reflect God's character and keep a spirit of reconciliation at the heart of political disagreements with our brothers and sisters in Christ.

The things that divide us are about us; the things that unite us are about Him.

(Happy ending note: McLean Bible Church is thriving as a beacon for the Gospel, both locally in the Washington, D.C., area and among the nations. And David Platt's insightful book, *Before You Vote*, was a critical resource that helped shape my thinking around these issues.)

Politics in the Pulpit

I'm not a pastor. As far as I'm concerned, no amount of stress in the White House or intelligence community could compare to the weight of shepherding the eternal souls of people God had entrusted to a pastor's care. But my grandfather and my father were both pastors, and so I know firsthand that even the most hard-fought political campaigns rarely get any nastier than the criticism, frustration, and vitriol that are sometimes aimed at pastors from members of their own congregations!

The last thing pastors need is another armchair quarterback telling them how to do their jobs. So anything I have to say about how pastors should lead their churches is coming from a place of great humility and appreciation. And it's shaped by my perspective as someone who straddles the great divide between the church, American politics, and the media. In other words, I have a viewpoint, but I know the view from any church pew isn't the same as the view from behind the pulpit.

One of the most important jobs any leader has is deciding what issues—of the seemingly infinite number that exist—to elevate and bring to the attention of their followers. Pastors must rely on the Holy Spirit's guidance to navigate the inputs that influence their decision-making around sermon topics, including the input of their media consumption. The reason is that what's driving the political news cycle shouldn't be the driving force behind pastors' sermon choices, although it's also not completely irrelevant.

Pastors must be shepherds first and teachers second.

If pastors feel led to speak God's truth into the political and cultural issue of the day, they must take pains to understand all of the different angles. To give a specific example, consider the Black Lives Matter protests that spread to cities around the United States in the summer of 2020.

Racism is abhorrent and it is antithetical to the Gospel. And during that time well-meaning Christian leaders from around the United States preached powerful sermons on racial reconciliation. Some even participated in marches, standing with Christian brothers and sisters of all races to celebrate John's vision of heaven in Revelation 7, which includes Christians "from every nation, from all tribes and peoples and languages."

However, all of these good, Gospel-centered intentions were undermined by the reality that the Black Lives Matter organization was openly and actively advocating for issues that are antithetical to biblical Christianity.

On the BLM website, for example, the group stated they were "committed to disrupting the Western prescribed nuclear family structure requirement." But this so-called "Western prescribed"[2] structure is actually the one created by God—the same one Paul wrote about in Ephesians 5 to be modeled after Christ's relationship with the church, for whom he laid down his life.

BLM also proclaimed its mission to "dismantle cis-gender privilege and uplift Black trans folk,"[3] placing the organization at the forefront of the gender revolution that stands completely at odds with God's beautiful design for all of humanity: "So God created man in his own image, in the image of God he created him; male and female he created them" (Genesis 1:27).

Now, I agree with pastor Rick Warren, who said, "Our culture has accepted two huge lies. The first is that if you disagree with someone's lifestyle, you must fear or hate them. The second is that to love someone means you agree with everything they believe or do. Both are nonsense."[4]

However, pastors who feel led to provide much-needed spiritual guidance to their congregations in order to make Biblical sense of hot-button political and cultural issues must:

1. Take the time to understand the political and cultural nuances, and
2. Not mimic the approach of political pundits who present convenient facts and ignore the difficult or uncomfortable ones.

Transporting ourselves back to the summer of 2020, the murder of George Floyd, the subsequent riots, and the BLM movement in general were being discussed and debated at office water coolers and dinner tables around the country. It could potentially make sense for a pastor to pause a planned sermon series to address these issues.

In that moment, pastors who allowed fear of pushback to prevent them from preaching that racism is an evil that God hates, and that the church should be a picture of the unifying power of Christ across racial and ethnic boundaries, were wrong. But it was also wrong for pastors to ignore or gloss over the anti-Biblical agenda that BLM and other groups were subversively trying to advance as part of their movement, often using the racial issue as a smokescreen. Addressing either one of those issues without the other could, at best, if done out of ignorance, leave the congregation confused; and at worst, if done out of fear or intentional omission, expose the pastor to justifiable allegations of advancing a political agenda himself.

Pastors shouldn't program their sermons like they're programming the nightly news. "If it bleeds, it leads" should only apply to Christ's death, burial, and resurrection and the fact that his blood is the only payment that could cover all our sins. That should be at the forefront of everything. In a politics-obsessed culture and media environment, letting the media and culture drive sermon topics or content will by definition result in politics supplanting the Gospel as the focus of the message.

God's word is transcendent, true for all time and at all times. So rather than trying to shoehorn the gospel into commentaries on the issues of the day, it's a lot more effective to preach scripture boldly and consistently, without fear of—but also without ignorance of—the implications in the culture.

Ultimately there is no blanket right or wrong answer when pastors should use the pulpit to address political or cultural issues of the day, but wise pastors will have a decision-making framework that includes trusted inputs and ensures outcomes that edify the church and keep the Gospel in the preeminent place it deserves. Bottom line: Don't let politics or fear decide what gets preached.

Politics and Purpose

Gary Palmer is quietly one of the most influential members of Congress. As chairman of the House Republican Policy

Committee, Gary helps shape the Republican agenda in the House and has a voice in some of the most significant policy debates. He also happens to be my congressman and my neighbor.

In 2023, I was in Washington, D.C., the same week as the State of the Union Address, so Gary invited me to tag along as his guest. I gorged myself on the buffet in the speaker of the House's office and got a kick out of being the only person within ten miles of the Capitol who wasn't wearing a suit that night. However, much more interesting than President Biden's snooze-fest of a speech was the meeting that Gary invited me to attend the following morning.

While most of D.C. was sleeping off their post–State of the Union hangover—some literally, others figuratively—Gary and about a half dozen other members of Congress huddled for prayer and Bible study in one of their offices near the Capitol.

I listened as they read and discussed scripture, considered ways it applied to their jobs and personal lives, recalled conversations over the last week when they were able to weave in Gospel threads in conversations with their colleagues, acknowledged missed opportunities they hoped to get again, and encouraged each other to keep being a light in what can sometimes be a very dark and lonely place for a Christian.

Congress is so unpopular that its approval rating sometimes dips into the single digits, and deservedly so. Many of its members earn their reputations for being self-centered, self-serving, power-hungry demagogues. But over the course of about an hour that morning, God softened my heart and changed my perception of Congress, at least in one specific way. I saw the members who wake up before dawn and gather together for the sake of making the Gospel known in the mission field to which God has sent them: the halls of power.

They weren't looking to score political points with the Christian, conservative base. They weren't beating their chests and drawing attention to themselves. They were in their metaphorical prayer closet. Were it not for me writing about it here, no one would really even know that outside of the spotlight, quietly, without seeking recognition, they were being faithful. And they told me there were more of them who weren't there that morning, or who were holding similar meetings at different times.

There is hope for our government, not because we put our hope in any government, but because there are members of our government whose hope is in Christ.

One of the reasons why historically it has been easy to be a Christian in America is because our nation's laws have been very much in line with what our Founders called "the laws of nature and of nature's God." The more that is the case, the more just our society will be. That's worth fighting to preserve and perfect.

But while we should expect a lot from our elected representatives and hold them accountable for their conduct and performance in office, no politician should occupy the central place they often do in our power- and-celebrity-crazed culture.

In one sense, Jesus is history's greatest political revolutionary. He took away—for all of eternity—the ultimate power of every would-be tyrant: the power over life and death, the power to "win" by killing their enemies. As Jesus said in Matthew 10, we have no reason to "fear those who kill the body but cannot kill the soul." This is why the Christian faith is a threat to authoritarian regimes that rule through force and intimidation and why churches are kept firmly under the thumb of the government in places like China. Communist regimes don't want anyone getting the bright idea that God could replace the state in their hearts and minds.

But while God has the power to "remove kings and raise up kings" (Daniel 2:21), Jesus did not die for the purpose of conquering earthly tyrants. John 6 is a famous chapter in the Bible because it includes the story of Jesus feeding the five thousand with five loaves of bread and two fish. One of the lesser remembered verses from that chapter, but a significant one, comes after Jesus' miracle left the people blown away by what they had witnessed: "Perceiving then that they were about to come and take him by force to make him king, Jesus withdrew again to the mountain by himself" (John 6:15).

The people wanted a revolutionary to lead their overthrow of the Romans, but instead of conquering an earthly regime, Jesus conquered sin and death and created a pathway to reconciliation with God. This is the good news of the Gospel: "God shows his love for us in that while we were still sinners, Christ died for us."

Jesus' death and resurrection are the most important events in all of human history. Tiberius was the emperor of Rome and

Pontius Pilate was the governor of Judea when these events took place, but they were not the central characters in the story—Jesus was. And he still is.

So why on Earth would we make politicians the central characters in our story today?

ACKNOWLEDGMENTS

This book began as a labor of love and personal exploration long before it had any prospect of being something anyone else might read. I'm occasionally reminded of Jesus' words in Mark 6:4, "A prophet is not without honor, except in his hometown and among his relatives and in his own household." I'm clearly no prophet, but I am thankful for my wife, Megan, who, in spite of enduring my innumerable flaws, has never made me feel unworthy to do something so seemingly presumptuous as writing a book about "faith lessons" learned from our journey together.

I also want to thank my son, Shep, who is still too young to understand why Daddy was stuck typing on the computer for hours instead of wrestling in the living room. I have dedicated this book to you, and as you grow up, you should know how influential the extraordinary experience of being your dad was in so many of its entries—and in deepening my faith.

Thank you to Matt Latimer at Javelin for being both the world's greatest literary agent and a great friend through our many adventures (and bank heists!) together.

Thank you to Ryan Peterson, Beth Adams, and Daisy Hutton at Hachette Nashville for believing in this book's concept and in its ability to have a meaningful impact on the world. And to their marketing colleagues Canaan Byrd, Catherine Hoort, Patsy Jones, Ellie Long, Kaitlin Mays, and Katie Robison for making sure it reached the widest possible audience.

A very special thank-you to my mom, Brenda Sims, who improved this book immensely with her serious editing skills.

I also must express my sincere appreciation for the resource ministries of John Piper and David Platt (*Desiring God* and *Radical*, respectively) for being indispensable research assets throughout this process.

NOTES

Prologue

1. "Modeling the Future of Religion in America," Pew Research Center, September 13, 2022. https://www.pewresearch.org/religion/2022/09/13/modeling-the-future-of -religion-in-america/.

2. Jeffrey M. Jones, "U.S. Church Membership Falls Below Majority for First Time," Gallup, March 29, 2021. https://news.gallup.com/poll/341963/church-membership -falls-below-majority-first-time.aspx.

Author's Note

1. "Mississippi Sniper Kills 1, Wounds Several," *Washington Post*, n.d. https://www .washingtonpost.com/archive/politics/1996/04/13/mississippi-sniper-kills-1-wounds -several/86ac5f6a-559d-4949-9719-711ae618352b/.

Chapter 1: The Wilderness: Anxiety, Uncertainty, & God's Plan

1. John Anderer, "Land of the Worried: 83% of Americans Very Stressed Over Nation's Future," StudyFinds.org, June 19, 2020. https://www.studyfinds.org/land-of-the -worried-83-of-americans-very-stressed-over-nations-future/.

2. Tamar Lapin and Jackie Salo, "Upcoming Pentagon Report Will Detail 'Difficult to Explain' UFO Sightings," *New York Post*, March 22, 2021. https://nypost.com/2021/03/21 /pentagon-report-will-detail-difficult-to-explain-ufo-sightings/.

3. Paul David Tripp, *New Morning Mercies: A Daily Gospel Devotional* (Crossway, 2014), entry for February 18.

4. Jobs, Steve. "Steve Jobs Secret of Life," Silicon Valley Historical Association. https://www.youtube.com/watch?v=kYfNvmF0Bqw.

Chapter 2: The Way: Work, Culture Wars, & Counting the Cost

1. Michael Dobbs, "The Real Story of the 'Football' That Follows the President Everywhere," *Smithsonian* magazine, October 2014. https://www.smithsonianmag.com /history/real-story-football-follows-president-everywhere-180952779/.

2. Robert G. Ingersoll, *Abraham Lincoln, A Lecture* (New York: C. P. Farrell, 1895), p. 52. https://archive.org/details/abrahamlincolnle00inge/page/52/mode/2up.

3. John Piper, "Money, Sex, and Power: The Dangers," desiringGod, June 27, 2015. https://www.desiringgod.org/messages/money-sex-and-power-the-dangers.

4. Stephen Benedict Dyson and Charles A. Duelfer, "Assessing How the U.S. Intelligence Community Analyzes Foreign Leaders," *International Journal of Intelligence and CounterIntelligence* 33, no. 4 (2020): 768–796. https://www.tandfonline.com/doi/full/10 .1080/08850607.2020.1733544?scroll=top&needAccess=true.

5. Robert Windrem, "How the CIA Diagnoses World Leaders from Afar," NBC News, August 3, 2006, https://www.nbcnews.com/id/wbna14173327.

6. Jack Newman, "'There Is No Happiness in Life, Only a Mirage of It on the Horizon': Vladimir Putin Quotes Tolstoy as He Reveals His Dark Philosophy on Life and Inspires More Bond Villain Comparisons after Summit with Joe Biden," Mail Online, June 16, 2021, https://www.dailymail.co.uk/news/article-9694027/Vladimir-Putin-channels-inner -Bond-villain-saying-no-happiness-life-mirage.html.

7. For further study, read Matthew 6.

8. Jerry Dunleavy, "Intelligence Analysts Downplayed Chinese Election Influence to Avoid Supporting Trump Policies, Inspector Finds," *Washington Examiner*, January 7, 2021, https://www.washingtonexaminer.com/news/intelligence-analysts-downplayed-elec tion-interference-trump-inspector.

9. Lewis, C. S., "The Inner Ring," Memorial Lecture at King's College, University of London, 1944. https://www.lewissociety.org/innerring/#:~:text=Unless%20you%20 take%20measures%20to,you%20of%20its%20own%20accord.

Chapter 3: The (Great Com)Mission

1. McNeil, Jeffery, "From the Crack House to the White House," *Street Sense*, March 7, 2018, https://www.streetsensemedia.org/article/white-house-homeless-writer -trump-supporter-street-paper/.

2. "Which is the Chattier Gender?" University of Arizona, July 2, 2007. https://news .arizona.edu/story/which-chattier-gender.

3. Carson, D. A., *Memoirs of an Ordinary Pastor*, Crossway, February 5, 2008.

Chapter 4: The Valley: Suffering, Weakness, Persecution, and Grace

1. Sophia Marie Campa-Peters (@ninjakittensophia), Instagram, https://www .instagram.com/ninjakittensophia/?hl=en.

2. Julia La Roche, "Goldman Sachs' 2nd-most-powerful executive pulled an audacious move to get his 1st job on Wall Street," *Business Insider*, June 1, 2015, https://www .businessinsider.com/how-goldman-gary-cohn-got-to-wall-street-2015-5.

3. "9 Insults That Make the Presidential Campaign Seem Civilized," Merriam-Webster.com, n.d., https://www.merriam-webster.com/words-at-play/are-presidential -campaigns-getting-nastier-not-really/hermaphroditical.

Chapter 5: The Journey: Purpose in Everyday Life

1. For more on this, read *How Do You Kill 11 Million People?* by Andy Andrews (Thomas Nelson, 2012).

2. Albert Mohler, "Why Darwinism Survives," Albertmohler.com, January 17, 2006, https://albertmohler.com/2006/01/17/why-darwinism-survives.

3. If you're interested in going deeper, read Lee Strobel's *The Case for a Creator* (Zondervan, 2004).

Chapter 6: The Collision: Faith and Politics

1. Dave Boyer, "David Platt, McLean Bible Church pastor, apologizes for praying for Donald Trump, *Washington Times*, June 3, 2019, https://www.washingtontimes.com/news/2019/jun/3/david-platt-mclean-bible-church-pastor-apologizes-/.

2. Alex Nitzberg, "Black Lives Matter's Agenda Is about More Than Race," *The Hill*, September 6, 2016, https://thehill.com/blogs/pundits-blog/civil-rights/294451-black-lives-matter-agenda-is-about-more-than-race/.

3. Ibid.

4. Alex Murashko, "Exclusive Rick Warren: 'Flat Out Wrong' That Muslims, Christians View God the Same," *Christian Post*, March 2, 2012, https://www.christianpost.com/news/exclusive-rick-warren-flat-out-wrong-that-muslims-christians-view-god-the-same-70767/.

ABOUT THE AUTHOR

Cliff Sims served as Deputy Director of National Intelligence for Strategy and Communications, working in the office that produces the President's Daily Intelligence Brief (PDB) and oversees the eighteen agencies of the U.S. intelligence community. In this role, Mr. Sims was awarded the Director's Exceptional Achievement Award in recognition of superior accomplishment and valuable service to the mission of the Office of the Director of National Intelligence.

Mr. Sims was previously Special Assistant to the President and Director of White House Message Strategy under President Trump. In this role, he had an office in the West Wing and led the White House's messaging operation, advising the president and senior officials on communications strategy. Mr. Sims spearheaded communications for some of the administration's most notable accomplishments, including the successful passage of the Tax Cuts and Jobs Act, the most significant tax cut and reform package in a generation.

Team of Vipers, a memoir of his time in the White House, became an instant *New York Times* bestseller. He also led the messaging and speechwriting team for the 2020 Republican National Convention.

In the private sector, Mr. Sims was the founding CEO of Yellowhammer Multimedia, an influential Alabama-based media company that published *Yellowhammer News* and syndicated the Yellowhammer News Radio Network. He sold the company upon accepting a position in the White House. He was also the CEO of Telegraph Creative, a full-service marketing, advertising and creative firm with clients ranging from multinational corporations to small businesses and startups, to government agencies. He sold his ownership stake in the company in 2023.

Through his strategic advisory firm, C. D. Sims & Co., Mr. Sims leverages his experience from the Oval Office to the corner office and the Situation Room to the board room, to help clients manage risk, navigate crises, and enhance their brands. He has appeared on Fox News, CNN, MSNBC, CBS, and ABC, and his opinions on national security, foreign policy, and current events have been published in *The Wall Street Journal, The New York Times, Newsweek, The National Interest,* and numerous other publications.

Mr. Sims graduated Magna Cum Laude from the University of Alabama with a bachelor's degree in political science and received an Executive Certificate in Public Leadership from Harvard University's John F. Kennedy School of Government. He now lives in Birmingham, Alabama, with his wife, Megan, and their six-year-old son, Shep. The Simses are members of The Church at Brook Hills.